Home MAGAZINE | A FAMILY HOME

Home MAGAZINE A FAMILY HOME

Designs for the Way We Live Today

GALE C. STEVES
Editor-in-Chief, Home® Magazine

Text by
JIM KEMP

FRIEDMAN/FAIRFAX
PUBLISHERS

A FRIEDMAN/FAIRFAX BOOK

© 2000 by Michael Friedman Publishing Group, Inc.

Please visit our website: www.metrobooks.com

Library of Congress Cataloging-in-Publication Data

Kemp, Jim.
    Home magazine's A Family Home : designs for
    the way we live today / by Jim Kemp
        p.cm.
    Includes bibliographical references and index.
    ISBN 1-56799-872-0 (hardcover)
    1. Architecture, Domestic—United States
Designs and plans. 2. Architecture, Modern—
20th century—United States
Designs and plans. I.Home magazine. II.
Title. III. Title: A family home.

NA7205.K47 1999
643—dc21
                                99-20543

Special Thanks to Timothy Drew
Editor: Hallie Einhorn
Art Director: Jeff Batzli
Designer: Lori Thorn
Photography Editors: Wendy Missan and
Kathleen Wolfe
Production Manager: Karen Matsu Greenberg

Color separations by Dai Nippon
Printed in Hong Kong
by Dai Nippon Printing Company Limited

10 9 8 7 6 5 4 3 2 1

Distributed by Sterling Publishing Company, Inc.
387 Park Avenue South
New York, NY 10016
Distributed in Canada by Sterling Publishing
c/o Canadian Manda Group
One Atlantic Avenue, Suite 105
Toronto, Ontario, Canada M6K 3E7
Distributed in Australia by
Capricorn Link (Australia) Pty Ltd.
P.O. Box 6651
Baulkham Hills, Business Centre, NSW 2153,
Australia

CONTENTS

FOREWORD

Beyond simply providing shelter from the elements, homes through the centuries have always reflected the way people live. And from generation to generation, the way people live does change, sometimes a little, sometimes a lot. Few of us, for example, would be perfectly happy to move into Mount Vernon or Monticello—as lovely as both venerable residences may be—without thinking about what it would take to make these houses really suitable for our needs and wants today. As times change, so do our views of what our homes should offer.

Whether we are planning to remodel an older home, build a new house, or tour the model homes in a development that has recently sprung up, our wish lists are strong indicators of just how much the economy, social change, and technology have altered and expanded our expectations of what our homes should be. Two-income families are more the rule than the exception, and as often as not, children have their own involved activity schedules. In many ways, the home is a family command center that needs to function effortlessly and efficiently. Rather than creating obstacles and hurdles, a house should help ease our way through the day. We should not feel frantic in the morning because too many people need to use the same bathroom to get ready for work or school. And meal preparation should not be a hassle because the kitchen is poorly configured.

At the end of the day, the home also needs to offer a sense of refuge from the demands and stresses of the outside world. There needs to be a place to relax and interact with loved ones, a place where we can feel comfortable and be ourselves. Perhaps this is why the family room with an adjoining open kitchen enjoys such popularity. On a daily basis, this type of space allows family members to be together while focusing on individual tasks—preparing or helping with dinner, getting started on homework, or simply chatting about the day's activities. Of course, the concept of the multipurpose open family room/kitchen—or great room—is hardly new, but what is especially interesting is the extent to which we have embraced and adapted this idea to fit our needs.

Right: The area through which family members and guests come into your home should be welcoming. Even a humble mudroom can be turned into an inviting entry. Here, a closet not only stores outerwear, but greets visitors with a charming seaside scene and a colorful still life. The accommodating nature of the entry is heightened by the simple inclusion of a bench that offers a place to sit and remove boots. Thanks to a slate floor that can withstand any mud or water tracked in, the space is not only hospitable but practical.

And the great room is only one example of how our focus is changing. Although a new nomenclature hasn't yet emerged to describe some of the home's evolving spaces, today's homeowners don't feel bound by such traditional terminology as "dining room" or "living room." It's not that the dining room, for instance, is disappearing. As a separate room, it is, in fact, enjoying a renaissance, but as a dining space it is largely reserved for special occasions. On a day-to-day basis, we generally eat our meals in more informal settings, such as the kitchen or family room. But that doesn't mean that the formal dining room doesn't serve other purposes in between holidays and dinner parties. Outfitted with appropriate cabinetry or a handsome armoire to house computer equipment, the space can easily morph into a home office and then smoothly change back into an entertaining area when guests arrive.

Just as we value our gathering spaces, there are also times when family members want more privacy. Every household has its own requirements. Older children may need a quiet space away from the hubbub to settle down to homework or, on the other hand, room to entertain their own guests without unduly jangling their parents' nerves. Adults may savor a quiet den or perhaps the room formerly known as the living room for reading or for adult conversation away from the current episode of *Buffy the Vampire Slayer* showing in the family room.

As you read *A Family Home: Designs for the Way We Live Today*, I hope you will find ideas that you can adapt to your own needs. And just as importantly, I hope you will begin to see new possibilities for making your home work for you.

Gale C Steves

Editor-in-Chief, Home® Magazine

INTRODUCTION

We all have a working list of elements that would make up the perfect home, if not a complete vision of the ultimate dream house. And we add to that list every time we bump up against some aspect that doesn't seem to be right for us or the way we would like our families to live. It may be that the kitchen is poorly laid out or that when it's time to fix lunch or dinner, the designated cook is isolated from the rest of the family. And what about the bathroom? Is there a stress-inducing morning traffic jam guaranteed to get the day started off on the wrong foot? Room to be together with loved ones and friends is important, as is the availability of quiet spaces where we can relax and recharge our batteries.

Statistically speaking, the average house is thirty to forty years old. It was built before many of the conveniences and amenities that now seem commonplace were affordable or even widely available. Likely as not, a kitchen outfitted with a range, a refrigerator, and a bit of work space was deemed adequate, while a single bathroom for the entire family was the norm. What's more, the typical home predates by decades the explosion in electronics technology that has transformed how we use and enjoy our homes. Now we can program security systems, telecommute, and watch movies on our home theater systems. In a nutshell, most of us have a home that is from a different age.

As a result—and this will come as no surprise—we tend to lack the amount, type, and quality of space that we need for the way we live today. The kitchen is cramped and awkward. Bathrooms aren't large enough, or there are just too few of them. There's no place to set up shop and get some work done without completely disrupting the rest of the family. Equally unfortunate, the home is shut off from the outdoors and views of the natural world.

Transforming a residence into a beloved home is an age-old mission. Lucky is the family that can accomplish this feat by merely redecorating. For most of us, the task requires assessing individual and family needs for both the here and now and the future. Then it must be determined how those needs mesh with what the home currently provides. The result is usually a list of both shortcomings and superfluities—a point of departure that enables us to set goals and establish a timetable for reaching them.

A good way to start is by examining how you function in your home. You are likely to discover that in many ways

Right: Today's family home is much friendlier than its predecessors. Open planning brings the family together by eliminating unnecessary interior walls, allowing one member to read the paper while another cooks dinner and yet another sets the table.

you've compromised daily life to accommodate the physical limitations of the structure. Do family members start their day especially early—or late—so that they can bathe and groom uninterrupted by others? Have you resigned yourself to staying late at the office because there's no convenient place to work at home? Have you given up trying new, more elaborate recipes in your outdated, inefficient kitchen?

Your analysis will probably reveal the ways in which you have informally adapted your dwelling to become the home you need without even realizing it. Unfortunately, in most of these cases, the results are not particularly stylish. Is the breakfast bar the place where you open the laptop computer and spread out ongoing work projects? If so, you've created a home office, but unfortunately, it requires you to pack up work materials to make room for meal preparation. Is the foyer a mess with overcoats and raincoats thrown over chair arms and loose change, keys, and just plain "stuff" strewn across a table? In that case, you're keeping items in the general area where you need them, but you could create streamlined, out-of-the-way storage space by building a closet and incorporating a narrow hall table with drawers to hold odds and ends.

In some cases, minor adjustments can have major effects on the quality of home life. An excellent way to begin is to rework the space you already have. Some things are obvious, such as replacing small windows with larger ones, which helps bring house and site into harmony

With the kitchen, dining room, and living room all open to one another, no one ever feels isolated in this home. The space is packed with features that are fun and practical, such as an informal dining table that extends from the eat-in kitchen through the wall onto a deck (above). A window doubles as a handy pass-through. In the more formal dining space (left), a chandelier hangs above the table, lending the area an air of distinction. Although the dining "room" is only ten feet [33m] wide, it visually borrows space from the kitchen. But perhaps the most remarkable element is the massive wall of windows, which is actually a modified garage door (right).

and, at the very least, makes rooms seem bigger. Building window seats with drawers or cupboards and adding a closet underneath the stairs are easy ways to increase storage space. A spare bedroom that's empty most of the time is a perfect candidate for a home office. Attic space, particularly above the garage, is a prized location for a private media room. Of course, it can be put to equally good use as a craft and hobby workshop.

Sometimes, the answer is less apparent, such as removing the wall between the living room and kitchen to create a large family room. If yours is an informal clan, perhaps you'd like to take this idea one step further and consolidate the living and dining rooms as well as the kitchen into a great room, which would be the hub of family life. A seemingly unusable tiny bedroom adjacent to the master suite could become the biggest walk-in closet or dressing room in the neighborhood. It's just a matter of looking at the space you have in a fresh way.

For many, the solution to the need for more space is the building of an addition. A backyard deck, porch, or sunroom is a simple device for expanding functional living space for much of the year and linking your house to the outdoors. Many families feel the need to add a bathroom, a family room, and a master suite, which has spurred a type of addition that is enjoying immense popularity: the two-story variety placed at the side of a house. Usually, the family room is on the first floor, while the upper level contains a master bedroom suite—complete with a dressing room, a separate bath, and often a space-enhancing cathedral ceiling.

Left: Replacing solid walls with floor-to-ceiling windows makes even the smallest room seem bigger. Draperies or louvers can be used to control the amount of light admitted into the space, helping it to stay comfortable throughout the year. **Above:** A small space can be outfitted with a few basic furnishings to transform it into a home office. Here, glazed pocket doors keep the 9 x 9-foot [30 x 30m] room from feeling claustrophobic. At the same time, they contribute visual interest to both the work space and the adjacent living room.

These are just a few examples of what homeowners have always done—structured living spaces to be in sync with daily life, whether that requires adding rooms or rearranging existing ones. These days, however, you can achieve the same goals more thoughtfully and with better results. The development of new materials and space-planning ideas provides an unparalleled opportunity to tailor a house as thoroughly as a suit or dress. No longer must you accept someone else's idea of how to live and play. Nor are you consigned to "making do" by sacrificing style for convenience. You may not be able to have it all, but you can certainly turn the residence you have into a home you love.

CHAPTER ONE

COMING
AND GOING

Come on, now, tell the truth—how do you really enter your home? If you're like most people, you drive the car into the garage, get out, and walk into the kitchen. Equally important, how do guests come into your house? Do they enter through a side door into the family room or through a sliding glass door off the patio? Exactly who arrives through the formal front entry? For many, the answer is practically no one. As one designer put it, "only complete strangers come to the front door."

Yet we lavish plenty of attention on creating a formal entry that embodies the impression we're trying to make, whether it's one of formal elegance, casual appeal, or just plain welcoming warmth. We do this because we've been told for years that the entry deserves special care since it creates the first—and lasting—image of the home. Unfortunately, it seems the only people getting the message are those who are lost and seeking directions or those who want to sell us something. So who needs an entry? We do.

We need a place that serves as a transitional space between indoors and out. We need a place where we can lay down the newspaper and dump the mail. We need a place where we can leave keys, loose change, and all of the other flotsam and jetsam of everyday life that accumulates in our pockets. We need a place where we and our guests can shed and stash coats and umbrellas. Also, we need a bit of ceremony when we enter a home, something that denotes that we are moving from a public space into a private one. We need an entry.

But is a traditional foyer the answer? For more and more families, the foyer has become somewhat superfluous. In all too many cases, it's a superbly decorated—and barely used—little jewel of a space. It has a half-bath that's eternally spick-and-span and a coat closet that's either empty or stuffed with out-of-season clothing.

Most families lead a fairly casual home life, which makes the traditional foyer a room that's basically in the wrong place. If your family and friends tend to enter your house through the back door, the side door, or even the

We need a bit of ceremony when we enter a home, something that denotes that we are moving from a public space into a private one.

Pages 14–15: Most of us walk into our houses through a side or back entry, so why not make these spaces appealing? In this case, the homeowners created not only a friendly entrance, but a gardening room as well. A durable tile floor stands up to rain and snow, and an abundance of glass lets the sun indoors. On the decorative front, beadboard cabinet doors, old-fashioned hardware, and a vintage-style faucet infuse the space with a sophisticated country tone. In front of the window, a sack-back Windsor chair provides a comfortable spot for removing winter wear or putting on boots. **Opposite:** The dark and dreary foyer is a thing of the past. Emphasizing a light and airy look, today's entry can serve as a sunroom or mini-greenhouse. Here, the effect is achieved with an overscale doorway incorporating lots of glass.

Right: Because it was always the entry of choice, a back porch off the kitchen was designed to serve as a worthy prelude to the rest of the home. The delightful light-filled entrance gets its charm from simple but carefully chosen elements, including a restful shade of purple for the walls, a painted wooden bench, a delicate white birdcage (hanging overhead), and an airy plant stand filled with fresh greenery. An inviting table at the end of the space speaks of hospitality and beckons family members and guests onward.

Opposite: This mudroom located at the back of the house was transformed into an accommodating entrance with the incorporation of built-in benches and an overhead shelf that provides display space as well as hooks for hanging jackets. Just like the more lived-in areas of the home, the entrance has been decorated with a certain motif in mind. A garden theme comes across in the bench cushions, the matching curtains, the watering cans, and the window box. **Above:** A foyer whose decor takes its inspiration from the Arts and Crafts Movement contains all of the storage any modern home needs. The compact but gracious space includes a Stickley coatrack, an umbrella stand, and a handsome table featuring drawers and shelves. A small but carefully selected assortment of collectibles provides a welcoming touch.

garage, it's time to synchronize design with reality and relocate the entry to the appropriate spot. Many houses already have a mudroom separating the kitchen from the outdoors. Some even include a half-bath that can be upgraded to a powder room for guests. If a half-bath is not present, there still may be water lines intended for a laundry machine. Such an area can be converted into a half-bath, and the washer and dryer can be relocated conveniently closer to the master suite.

If there's room, add a closet for stowing long coats, scarves, hats, umbrellas, and that old jacket you wear when you walk the dog. Or hang coats out in the open on wall pegs, a convenient storage strategy that also reinforces informal decorating schemes, such as the ever-popular country look.

Pre–World War II houses usually have a small service porch that can be enclosed and transformed into a year-round backyard entry. A less expensive alternative is to set off the porch by adding screening or decorative latticework. A breezeway linking the kitchen and garage can be remodeled into an enclosed entry, which will increase protection from intruders.

If your house doesn't already have a service porch, a similar effect can be created by adding a sunroom. The beauty of such an addition is that it blends the best of the outside and the inside—a warm, sunny area with complete protection from the elements. Besides increasing living space, a properly sited sunroom helps heat your home by collecting the free warmth of the sun on clear—even if cold—days.

Some people take advantage of a foyer for storage and display space. By now, everyone has seen photographs of foyers where pegs support a collection of interesting hats. A musician put his foyer to better use by designing a storage unit with doors that conceal cubbyholes for his instruments, music stands, and sheet music. One woman, an avid shoe-shopper, hired a carpenter to build a low cabinet with several shelves for shoes. The woman placed a chair nearby, allowing her to sit and take off expensive dress shoes upon arriving home from work and immediately stash them away. Similarly, the setup enabled her to put them on just before leaving.

In some homes, especially those built in the 1950s and 1960s, the foyer has been eliminated entirely. People entering through the front door in this sort of home walk directly into the living room. There's no standing on ceremony. The problem in these houses is how to create an actual entry—or at least a sense of one.

If such a dwelling already has a front porch, extending the house outward with a new front porch and incorporating the old one into the living space is one way to go. Another effective solution is to carve out a foyer within the existing living space. For example, building floor-to-ceiling closets adjacent to the front door creates a definitive passageway into the room and provides the necessary storage space for outerwear. You can distinguish the entry even more by lowering the ceiling. With this approach, guests feel the impact of moving from the public realm into a private space, thanks to the relative intimacy of the entry area. Substituting glass-block walls also provides a sense of entry, with the added bonus of promoting the uninhibited flow of light.

One family achieved this effect by building a translucent wall several feet into the living room, which basically divided one room into two. Although they were concerned the wall would establish an unwelcome, cramped atmosphere in the living area, the change ended up having the opposite effect. Graced with a view of the new entry, which was painted a bit darker, the living room now seems larger than it did prior to the remodeling.

Before making any permanent changes, experiment. For instance, place tall folding screens where you are thinking of building closets. Living with this arrangement for a week or so will help you decide whether you want to proceed with the initial plan. The folding screen itself may turn out to be the solution you're looking for, especially if you add containers of colorful houseplants and a tall hat stand.

Above: Though it's narrow, this side entrance seems as vast as the outdoors, thanks to a generous use of glass on the doors and an interior wall of windows. With easy-clean tile flooring and a built-in unit boasting deep drawers, the space is both inviting and serviceable. **Right:** In some cases, the simple addition of a partial wall is all it takes to convert an ungainly space into a relaxed foyer. Here, such a wall has been accented with a pair of columns to introduce a bit of ceremony. To further enhance the appeal of the setting, the wall between the entry and the living room has been fitted with transom-like windows that allow light to flow freely between the two areas. Nestled into a corner by the door, a plant-filled multitiered stand not only takes advantage of the sunshine streaming through the sidelight, but also warms up the space.

With some brainstorming, you're certain to establish an entry that suits both your traffic patterns and your personal style.

Opposite and above: Thanks to a wise use of space, this entrance not only serves up a hearty welcome, but also acts as a potting shed and a home office. The flagstone floor stands up to heavy traffic, soil, and splashes of water while enhancing the naturalistic mood of the setting. While the garden task areas are streamlined against one wall, the office setup is poised to take advantage of a bank of windows. Garden accessories and tools hung on the walls and displayed on shelves become eye-catching decorative accents.

Whether your entry is permanent or temporary, or located at the front, rear, or side of your home, you'll want to decorate it so that guests feel welcome. An austere entry painted in cold decorator-white and lacking any personal touches sets completely the wrong mood. It's as though anyone, or perhaps no one, lives in the home.

Adding a personal touch is easy if your preferred decorating scheme is traditional, eclectic, country, or the popular cottage style. An antique hall stand supplies sufficient storage space for guests' wraps while imbuing the entry with old-fashioned charm. Laying down an antique runner will have a similar effect on the tone. One woman created just the right mood by arranging her collection of mirrors on the entryway wall, which also made the space seem larger.

Though contemporary design schemes emphasize sparseness, a properly sized, framed mirror can be exactly the right decorative accent, as it will create the illusion of more space. It is also a nice courtesy to guests, enabling them to deal with "hat hair" and the like. To emphasize the mirror, flank it with modern sconces. Or, if you prefer, simply include a ready-made peg rack–cum-mirror, where guests can shed their coats and primp at the same time. A classically inspired console table offers space to set down packages and brings a bit of eclecticism into an otherwise contemporary room. A bowl of fresh flowers, either in an array of colors or in a monochromatic vein, is a thoughtful way of letting guests know you are happy to have them in your home.

Usually, an entry is illuminated by an overhead light fixture in the appropriate size and style. With the installation of a rheostat, you can establish different degrees of brightness for various occasions. For a different touch, substitute a table lamp for a suspended fixture. This works well in informal decorating schemes and is superbly suited to back or side entries, which are inherently casual.

With some brainstorming, you're certain to establish an entry that suits both your traffic patterns and your personal style. It's just a matter of evaluating your needs and doing a little creative thinking.

CHAPTER TWO

GATHERING

What a difference a century makes! At this time one hundred years ago, the typical home was divided into a rabbit's warren of rooms. The gathering area—namely the parlor and, later, the formal living room—was an uncomfortable, be-on-your-best-behavior space. Needless to say, it did little to promote family togetherness.

Nowadays, we spend much of our time in a space that didn't even exist back then—the family room—or in a hybrid space called the living-dining room. Why? The design of new homes changed dramatically after World War II. In part to reduce construction costs, architects threw in the towel on the separate living room, combining it with the dining room to form a single rectangular or L-shaped space. This blending of rooms became known as open planning. No longer was a room assigned one specific purpose and closed off from other areas; instead, spaces were unified and put to multiple uses.

Besides cutting building costs, open planning yielded a gathering room that, at the time of its inception, was twice as big as the individual rooms to which people were accustomed. And though the size of the typical postwar home was not significantly different from that of its predecessors, it seemed much larger.

The postwar era also marked the beginning of adapting homes to meet our needs instead of altering our living patterns to accommodate the confines of the structure. For example, the TV room debuted in the 1950s. From there, it evolved into the den or rumpus room before flowering into the modern family room.

Some large, new "executive" homes still include a separate living room, but it is a mere shadow of its former self.

Pages 24–25: This restful living area lets in the light with numerous windows, large and small. Glass-paned doors open onto a deck, expanding the living space both visually and physically. While a coffee table, a plump chair, and an overstuffed sofa encourage folks to gather around, a cozy alcove complete with built-in cushioned seating beckons those who desire a little quiet time away from the center of the action.

Above: One type of open-plan design that fulfills a number of functions is the great room. With areas for cooking, dining, and just plain relaxing, the space offers something for everyone. Although the different parts of this great room clearly serve different purposes, they are unified by the overall lodgelike ambience. **Opposite:** In an open-plan room, the easiest way to define activity areas is with furniture groupings. Here, a table and seating in front of a window create a bright, informal dining area, while a rug subtly marks the sitting area.

Today, the formal living room is often nothing more than a token tribute to the past—a small space cut off from most family activities and about as useful as an appendix. Indeed, in many cases, its only purpose is to serve as a display arena for Christmas gifts.

Since living-dining and family rooms seem to be part and parcel of today's homes, it's difficult to imagine a residence without one or the other. Both are all-purpose rooms where we relax after work, play with the youngsters, screen movies, and/or watch television. They are the nerve centers of teenagers' school projects one day and playgrounds for the preschool set the next. These activity hubs are where we dine casually, even on formerly formal holidays. And they are where we entertain friends in a relaxed setting—from a quiet kaffeeklatsch to a Sunday afternoon congregation of rambunctious sports fans.

Left: Child-size chairs arranged around a low but large coffee table allow children to feel that the family room belongs to them, too. The setup provides a great spot for snacks, games, and craft projects. Off to the side, a windowed alcove creates a sunny and somewhat separate retreat for the grown-ups while allowing them to keep close watch over activities in the other part of the room. **Right:** The attic can become a magical gathering place for kids. Here, an imaginative architect designed enough built-in units to supply storage space for an entire kingdom. A niche outfitted with window seats creates an intimate spot for story hour, and a small table and chairs offer the perfect setting for a tea party. There's even a blackboard built into one of the storage units, encouraging children to unleash their creative talents.

If you live in a prewar home, a family room was probably added long ago, or you may be planning to build one of your own. Before you go to that expense, though, study your residence analytically. It may already have the necessary space split up among several rooms. Think how you can consolidate these areas into the room that you want. You may be able to knock down a wall or two instead of adding a completely new space.

As you rethink your home, look for room for an extra gathering place. Designers have long situated comfortable chairs on a stair landing or in a wide hallway to create a small conversation area. Instead of keeping a breakfast area that is utilized only once a day, convert it into an intimate den. It's easy! Remove the chandelier, if the breakfast area has one, and replace the dining table and chairs with sink-into seating and some storage units. Almost instantly you've "made" extra space to entertain a crowd or host the extended family. This setup also has the added bonus of opening onto the kitchen, where everyone tends to gravitate anyway.

In fact, the family room has become even more of an attraction in recent years by annexing the kitchen. Though this great room, as it is called, conjures up images of a Tudor-era banquet hall, it's a perfect model for the way most people live today. Incorporating the kitchen into the living-dining area keeps whoever is cooking in the midst of family activities. No longer shut off in a separate room, an adult or adolescent can visually monitor young children in the living area, take part in family chatter, or watch the television news while boiling pasta for dinner.

Another gathering area that has become exceedingly popular is the media room. Outfitted with the latest in home-entertainment equipment, the media room is a place for family and friends to enjoy television, movies, and music without interruption. To ensure quiet (for both those using the room and those in the rest of the home), many families

Top: A wide landing should not be treated as dead space. This one has been put to good use as a quiet sitting area that projects the air of a library, thanks to its rolled-arm leather chairs and built-in bookcases. **Bottom**: The media room has developed into a popular gathering place for both family enjoyment and entertaining guests. One of the best locations is the attic space above the garage, which is secluded from the rest of the home. The soaring ceiling following the roofline enhances the sense of spaciousness, while a wall of storage keeps videotapes and compact discs organized. If space permits, you can include a few groupings of tables and chairs for playing board games and comfortably enjoying snacks.

As you rethink your home, look for room for an extra gathering place.

Above: Sitting areas can be mined out of all sorts of spaces. In this live-in kitchen, a built-in banquette outfitted with comfortable cushions encourages people to congregate and keep the cook company. Corner shelves filled with objects on display contribute to the living room character of the area.

Left: The living area in this great room gets its sense of intimacy from the orientation of the furnishings, which are grouped around an enticing wood-burning stove. On warmer days, when the stove is less of an attraction, the wall of French doors continues to encourage friends and family to gather and take in the view. Thanks to the open floor plan, the panoramic vista is shared by the dining space, which has been outfitted to coordinate with the living area.

are choosing to convert the attic area of the garage into a media room. This approach makes a lot of sense, as it takes advantage of an often underutilized space that is suitably off the beaten path. If your family enjoys renting a movie only occasionally, allow the garage attic to include other activities. It's a natural place to set up a Ping-Pong table as well as the family computer.

Despite their practicality, today's multifunctional gathering spaces can lack a necessary feeling of intimacy and privacy. Often, we desire a sense of separation between the different areas, either temporarily or permanently. Fortunately, it's quite easy to cut an open-plan room down to size—not by building walls, but by subtly dividing the space into smaller activity areas. It's no secret that the most common approach is to configure the furnishings into distinct groups according to function—for example, one group for sitting and one for dining. Using the same principle, you can break down a large living area into smaller, cozier conversation areas or into a television-watching area and a quiet conversation area. Heighten the sense of distinction through the strategic placement of area rugs, which will also provide visual warmth.

Interior designers have developed other techniques to tame the open-plan room. One method entails positioning sitting-area furniture around a fireplace, a wood-burning stove, or some other prominent architectural element. This type of feature automatically attracts people's attention, becoming the focal point of the room.

Create even more of an air of separation with a chest or some other low piece of furniture placed between activity spots. This useful strategy offers additional storage space without blocking the room-expanding view from one area to the other. You can also call upon color to distinguish different areas. Usually, this can be accomplished simply by specifying a darker tone for one area and a lighter tone of the same color for another.

Above: The vastness of this open-plan space is tamed in a variety of ways. A slight change in levels between areas contributes an air of distinction, which is reinforced by the strategic placement of low cabinets. Meanwhile, the boundaries between indoors and out are practically erased by skylights and a wall of glass reminiscent of a greenhouse.

Left: Stately columns are an effective device for marking the boundaries between different areas without going to the expense of constructing interior walls. Notice how the kitchen cabinetry pictured here has glass on both the front and back, thereby contributing to the open, spacious feeling of the first floor.

Interior designers have developed many techniques to tame the open-plan room. One method entails positioning sitting-area furniture around a fireplace, a wood-burning stove, or some other prominent architectural element.

Opposite: This cozy living room speaks of comfort and quiet pursuits. Fully stocked bookshelves line one wall, while two window seats invite lounging and reading. In the center of the room, furnishings are arranged to promote the easy flow of conversation, as well as to take advantage of the fireplace. **Right:** Besides supplying heat and acting as a focal point, a freestanding wood-burning stove can provide all the separation needed between a sitting area and a dining area. This example features compartments to stow logs, as well as surfaces for displaying decorative objects. A careful placement of rugs not only brings definition to the dining and gathering areas, but also injects warmth.

Remodeling or building an addition widens the options available to establish distinct activity areas in your gathering space. This is your opportunity to set one space a few steps lower than another—to create, for example, a sunken living room. Add that fireplace you've always wanted. Build bookcases along one or more walls to imbue a sitting area with a librarylike feeling. You'll be rewarded with a welcome bonus—additional storage space for a television set and a VCR as well as records, CDs, and tapes.

The opposite strategy is to make the outdoors the focal point of your gathering space. Punctuate an exterior wall with large windows, French doors, or a gliding patio door to transform an ordinary room into an enticing light-filled retreat. A row of skylights framing blue skies and white clouds extends the view up as well as out.

Many remodeling jobs include the addition of a sunroom or a greenhouse. Other renovations are visually distinguished by incorporating a wall of glass. Besides establishing a desirable focal point, directing people's gaze to the outdoors, these applications of glazing create vistas that make the interior seem larger than it really is.

Windows, doors, and other operable glass elements offer homeowners additional advantages. These features bring light indoors to brighten rooms throughout the year, even on overcast days. They also invite cool, refreshing breezes inside. When the weather is cold, modern refinements, such as insulated glass, help keep us comfortable without closing off exposure to the natural world.

Throughout our homes, we have made gathering spaces in—and out of—the most unlikely places. Besides reflecting our need to share each other's company, these areas demonstrate our creativity in tailoring our houses to conform to the way we want to live. Families one hundred years ago would be amazed by the relative informality of our lives at home and, perhaps, by the convenient arrangement and openness of our dwellings.

Punctuate an exterior wall with large windows, French doors, or a gliding patio door to transform an ordinary room into an enticing light-filled retreat.

Above: Imbuing this family room with twenty-four-hour appeal, a large window and a skylight harvest sunlight during the day and a fireplace emits a soft, golden glow at night. A sense of coziness is created by nesting the gathering area on its own level. **Opposite:** Instead of being just an architectural necessity, this staircase is an integral part of the living room's design. The effect has been achieved by transforming the space around the stairs into bookcases and display shelves.

CHAPTER THREE

DINING

Where at home do you eat dinner? The dining room, the kitchen, the family room, or some random makeshift spot? In all likelihood, your answer is all of the above. Today, an array of dining options is available—and it's a good thing. The sole-breadwinner household of a generation or two ago has been replaced by the dual-income family. Instead of the sit-down family dinners immortalized in the situation comedies of the 1950s—with jackets and ties, heels and pearls—today's meals tend to be somewhat impromptu affairs, prepared by whoever is available for whoever is home.

Although the dining room proper in most residences may sit empty except for holiday meals, there's a lot of resistance to give it up. In fact, the dining room appears to be enjoying something of a renaissance in home construction, thanks to baby boomers who want a special, elbows-off-the-table place that boasts a more formal tone than other parts of the home.

Below and right: An open-plan design allows a relaxed family room to flow into a casual dining area, which in turn flows into the kitchen. Simple wooden furnishings and blue-and-white checked upholstery contribute to the informal air of the space. While a breezy feeling unites the living-dining area and the kitchen work space, a lowered ceiling gently defines the two.

Pages 38–39: Options today range from the traditional formal dining room to various casual arrangements, such as a dining area located within the kitchen. In many cases, an island is the only means of separation between the meal preparation area and the dining space. Here, the use of wood for the cabinetry and island, a rack of gleaming copper pots, and a wood-beamed ceiling warm up the space, lending it a lived-in rather than utilitarian feel.

Adding cabinetry on both sides of—and above—a door in a dining room creates a particularly impressive effect while maximizing storage and display space.

Opposite: Architects and designers are enlivening the box-shaped dining room by adding windows, built-ins for storage, and decorative woodwork. Among old ideas being recycled for today's traditional-style homes are plate and chair rails and ceiling beams, all of which are often highlighted in contrasting colors. Open shelving shows off beautiful dishes, making them decorative objects in and of themselves, while a window seat contributes to the appeal of the room, offering a relaxed, out-of-the-ordinary spot to savor a cup of coffee. **Above:** In today's dining areas, you can have it all—an abundance of storage space and an abundance of natural light. Here, this magical feat has been accomplished by incorporating shelving above and around a generously sized window.

That doesn't mean your dining room has to be just like your mother's. The problem with the dining room of the past was that it tended to be boring. More often than not, it was an undistinguished, rectangular box, sometimes lacking any exposure to the outdoors.

Today, homeowners are remodeling their dining rooms by adding attractive moldings and other details that provide visual interest. One tactic is to install floor-to-ceiling built-in cabinetry. If glass-front doors are used, such cabinetry can show off a beautiful collection of china, allowing these pieces, which are probably only rarely used, to bask in the spotlight instead of being hidden away in some awkward, out-of-the-way spot where they do nothing but gather dust. Plus, this means of storage makes prized pieces readily available when a special occasion does arise, thereby doing away with the whole production of having to dig them out from behind other dishes in some inconvenient, difficult-to-reach kitchen cupboard.

Adding cabinetry on both sides of—and above—a door in a dining room creates a particularly impressive effect while maximizing storage and display space. Another practical and visually arresting design consists of two floor-to-ceiling storage cabinets flanking a waist-high center unit. With this configuration, the center portion can be used as a buffet and outfitted with drawers for flatware, linens, and other accessories. When not used as a serving counter, the top surface provides the perfect spot for a creative candle arrangement or some other intriguing display. Another way to make the dining room more alluring is to add a fireplace. This single change will draw family members of all ages—

not to mention guests—into the dining room, making it their preferred spot in which to eat and linger over after-dinner conversation.

More and more, the dining room is being remodeled so that it receives an increased amount of natural light. This goal is often accomplished via the installation of large replacement windows and glass doors. Along with creating a bright and airy atmosphere, glass opens up backyard views, making each meal a visual as well as gastronomic treat. Outfitting sliding glass doors with screens allows you to breathe in fresh air while savoring your meal, thereby creating an alfresco sensation in the dining room when weather permits.

Adding to the appeal of contemporary dining rooms is the variety of finishing treatments. For example, the floor is just as likely to consist of easy-care ceramic tile as traditional hardwood, thereby encouraging use of the space. A low-maintenance floor in the dining room makes eating there a less daunting prospect since you don't have to worry about potentially damaging spills. Regardless of the material, flooring is being set at an angle and embellished with inlaid designs. Ceilings are receiving more attention, too. Coffered and beamed ceilings are very much in vogue, especially when they are highlighted by recessed, cove, and low-voltage lighting fixtures.

Once you have transformed your dining room into an attractive, comfortable, and efficient space, don't reserve it for company alone. On those rare occasions when the whole family is home for dinner, try serving the meal in the dining room. Doing so will bring a little variety to the daily routine, and the pleasant ambience just might encourage some quality family bonding.

A fireplace will draw family members of all ages—not to mention guests—into the dining room, making it their preferred spot in which to eat and linger over after-dinner conversation.

Opposite: With an arched ceiling, an abundance of glazing, and an alluring fireplace, this dining room is an ideal milieu for entertaining. Glass-fitted doors invite family and guests to wander out to the patio between courses, while a fire sets the mood for lingering over dessert and coffee. **Right:** A far cry from the bland dining room of yesteryear, this space is packed with style. A grasscloth wallcovering with a checkerboard pattern gives the room a fresh but refined look, while a snazzy area rug with a variation on the checkerboard theme injects welcome color. The diagonally laid laminate flooring offers the elegant look of wood but is much easier to maintain.

Because informality rules our roosts these days, most of us take our meals in the family room or great room. Inherently casual, these rooms are perfect for unwinding after a hard day at work or school. Common sense dictates situating a family room's dining area close to the kitchen. This logical arrangement shortens the distance that food and dishes must be carried, thereby making the serving of meals easier and minimizing the chance of spills. Remember that the ultimate goal is to make less work for yourself, not more.

One type of dining spot that tends to be favored is a corner with windows on the two abutting walls. This setup

establishes an immediate sense of intimacy, which is enhanced by the beauty of natural light streaming indoors. A number of remodelings are taking the windowed corner a step further: large window units are arranged to create a three-sided bay for dining. The bay can be placed along any exterior wall, expanding the dining space and widening homeowners' design and decorating options.

A great room that includes a kitchen offers the advantage of a second eating area—the informal counter that separates the meal preparation area and the dining area. Adding a few comfortable stools or bar-height chairs extends the versatility of the counter, making it much more than just a spot to slice and dice. It is where children can grab a quick after-school snack, make a pit stop for lunch on a busy weekend, do homework, or simply hang out with mom and dad as they cook, giving family members an opportunity to spend more time together.

Left: In this eat-in kitchen, a harvest table has been paired with benches to imbue mealtime with the carefree spirit of a picnic. Low shelving units make the most of the space below the windows, providing plenty of room for storing cookbooks. In an area prone to spills, terra-cotta tile flooring offers practicality without sacrificing style.
Above: Situating a dining table so that it is enveloped by windows on three sides creates a cheery spot for meals. Here, a round table has been chosen to echo the curving lines of the surrounding architecture.

Left: This dining area conveys the laid-back feeling of French country style with its rush-seat ladder-back chairs and its upper walls painted in a hue that is suggestive of sun-baked earth. Beadboard wainscoting, highlighted in white, contributes to the provincial look and prevents the space from feeling heavy. A space-efficient corner cupboard holds decorative accents and an overflow of cookbooks from the adjacent kitchen.

Remember that the ultimate goal is to make less work for yourself, not more.

Right: The terra-cotta hue from the dining area is carried over into the kitchen, as is the material used for the floor. Resilient tile flooring works well with a variety of decorating schemes, and its cushioning gives bad backs a break. Everything about this kitchen—from the vintage advertisements hanging on the wall to the antique birdcage resting on the floor to the rabbit sculpture nestled at the foot of the island—demonstrates an awareness that this space is fully on view from the dining area.
Opposite: The kitchen is not only attractive, but highly efficient as well. A cobalt blue ceramic-tile backsplash, in keeping with the French country theme, enlivens a secondary work area, which includes a second sink. The cabinetry above features a built-in wine rack with the crisp look of latticework. A more formal dining room—separate but conveniently close to the kitchen—is visible through the doorway.

The space-dividing counter in a great room also facilitates having guests over. A neighbor can drop by and visit comfortably without disrupting ongoing work in the kitchen. In this day and age of multitasking, the host can smoothly entertain and cook at the same time. The counter also makes a handy serving surface for a casual buffet.

The most convenient place to dine, though, is within the kitchen. In fact, this has become such a popular spot for meals that in many new homes the in-kitchen eating area is getting larger, taking away space traditionally devoted

Below: In this open-plan home, the island performs a host of roles; it acts as a work surface, a dining spot, a storage device, and a divider. One of the benefits of an open floor plan is that light from one area is free to flow into the next. Here, the kitchen windows not only provide soft, indirect illumination for the dining area, but also pull double duty as display space thanks to an inventive incorporation of shelves.

Opposite: Strategically located for preparing food and enjoying quick meals, the center work island has become a mainstay of modern kitchen design. Luxurious yet durable surface treatments only add to its luster and appeal.

to the dining room. Architects and designers are dressing up the kitchen eating area in various ways. An appealing motif is the retro setup—a high-backed booth much like the kind you would find in an old restaurant. Another tried-and-true remedy is the incorporation of banquette seating against one or two walls, along with the addition of a table. This approach has proved so helpful in the remodeling of older homes that it is being taken a step further—a three-sided alcove that opens onto the meal preparation area and that can be outfitted with a dining table and either banquette seating or chairs.

The work island, now a standard component of modern kitchen design, originated as a small butcher block–topped table used to create extra work space. It has grown in size, importance, and purpose. One of its new functions is to serve as a surface for casual dining. Just like the counter separating the kitchen and dining areas in a great room, a center island can be furnished with stools for grabbing a quick meal or for enjoying a cup of coffee while scanning the morning headlines.

Above: Even the smallest kitchen can have an informal eating area. Here, the simple setup consists of two stools and a countertop beneath a window. In a real crunch, the counter can double as a place to do paperwork. **Right:** This retro-looking pedestal table and banquette combination resembles a cozy booth at a diner. Mirrors visually enlarge the space, preventing it from seeming claustrophobic, while wall sconces add a touch of elegance. A vaulted ceiling is painted with flowering vines, creating an alfresco feel.

Left: This dining niche has a seamless look, thanks to the way the base of the banquette matches the surrounding wainscoting. The primarily white milieu is accented with yellow and blue patterned cushions that not only offer loads of comfort but also give the space an upbeat tone.

Below: Instead of shoving a dining table against the end wall of a galley-style kitchen, why not increase the amount of seating with a banquette? Some versions even have drawers, providing storage space. Here, a sweep of glazing lends the sensation of dining outdoors.

Insulated glass harvests the warmth of the sun, which creates a comfortable dining area on even the coldest days, provided the sky is clear.

Opposite: A greenhouse addition need not be reserved for plants alone. This one serves as a colorful and fragrant setting for dining. Fitted with windows that open for ventilation, the space can be enjoyed during most of the year. Painting the framework white enhances the airiness of the space. **Right, top:** Soaring two stories high, this dining area takes center stage in the heart of the home. An area rug anchors the table in the midst of the vast open-plan space. **Right, bottom:** Placing an in-kitchen eating area front and center keeps diners from being relegated to a dark and dreary corner. Here, partial walls form a booth of sorts, creating the desired sense of intimacy without blocking the light from the windows. A more formal dining area is located just steps below.

You can dine "outdoors" throughout the winter with the help of a sunroom addition. Insulated glass harvests the warmth of the sun, which creates a comfortable dining area on even the coldest days, provided the sky is clear. At the same time, recent revolutionary improvements in glazing have reduced the amount of indoor heat lost to the outdoors. Proper positioning and venting of the addition minimizes the buildup of unwanted heat in the summer.

If you're not prepared to add a sunroom, you can brighten your dining area with skylights. These overhead windows to the treetops and sky are perfect for ushering natural light into a breakfast area or dining room that otherwise lacks exposure to the sun. They also open up a small space and make it seem less confined. Some types of skylights are composed of clear glass so that sunlight streams into the interior in bright shafts. Others, made with an opaque finish, illuminate the space with softly filtered light. Skylights are available in either operable or fixed versions. The operable variety opens in summer to exhaust hot air. The power that natural light, or a lack thereof, has upon our moods should not be underestimated.

Left and right: This fully equipped, expansive kitchen was created by merging a family room, a small kitchen, and a breakfast nook into one large space. In the process, three distinct dining areas were created. Casual meals and snacks can be had at either the peninsula in the front, which seats two, or the marble-topped center island, which doubles as a work surface. While Windsor chairs pull up to the peninsula, the island, which is higher, requires bar stools. A breakfast area at the rear of the kitchen offers a bright way to start the day with its stationary French doors and its octagonal skylight.

Right: By bringing in a one-of-a-kind view, whether of mountains or the ocean, windows imbue a dining area with a sense of place and context. Uninterrupted by mullions, these sheer expanses of glass blur the lines between indoors and out. Notice how the wood window frames and furnishings suit the landscape.

The power that natural light, or a lack thereof, has upon our moods should not be underestimated.

Left: Placing the dining area of an eat-in kitchen in a windowed alcove not only creates a sunny space for meals, but removes the table from the traffic pattern. Moreover, such a spot can make a hospitable home for a plant or two. Banquette seating is often used instead of chairs in order to increase the number of diners that can gather comfortably around the table.

Opposite: With sunlight pouring in from above and numerous plants providing lush greenery, this dining alcove feels as though it's outside. Natural materials, such as flagstone flooring, heighten the sensation. Even when no meal is being served, family members and guests are drawn to the bright area, which beckons them to bask in the sun.

CHAPTER FOUR

COOKING

Though it has become a cliché, the kitchen is the heart of today's home. Statistically speaking, it is the fastest growing room in new houses, increasing in size every year. Among home improvements, renovating the kitchen ranks as one of the top two projects (the other being the renovation of the bath). According to some estimates, more than four million kitchens are remodeled annually in the United States and Canada. Renovating can be an excellent investment. When homeowners sell, they can expect to get back, on average, 94 percent of the money spent on a good-looking cosmetic remodeling.

That we demand more from our kitchens is one reason we spend the money to make them bigger and better. We want additional appliances and amenities, such as a separate baking center. We want extra storage for cookbooks and exotic ingredients, and perhaps an under-the-counter refrigerator to hold bottles. Sometimes, we want the kitchen to accommodate a home office or laundry area as well.

Another impetus for renovating the kitchen is the desire to integrate it into a larger living space, such as a great room or open family room. Since in this situation the kitchen will be seen from other parts of the room, it is important that it fit in aesthetically with the overall space. For this reason, kitchen manufacturers are producing furniturelike cabinetry and surfacing materials that blend with all sorts of design schemes and styles. Taking this strategy a step further, some designers go with an "unfitted" kitchen, which replaces matching built-in wall-mounted cabinets with a variety of units and freestanding pieces of furniture to create a homey look.

Pages 60–61: This kitchen, which looks out onto a living area, keeps the cooks in constant contact with family members enjoying the other part of the open-plan room. An island divides the two, while a change in flooring—slatelike tiles for the kitchen, carpeting for the gathering area—heightens the distinction. Highly practical, the island features a small cooktop right beside the sink so that heavy pots filled with water don't have to travel far.

Above: Off the beaten path, this home office is located in a kitchen's secondary task area. A beautiful view of the outdoors is a welcome treat for those hard at work. The more kitchen-oriented features include a second sink and under-counter bottle storage. **Right:** The primary work area of the kitchen boasts an abundance of storage; a work island that can be used for preparing food, doing homework, or serving informal meals; and a refrigerator that blends into the surrounding cabinetry. The bright color scheme unites the kitchen and the adjoining dining room, making both seem larger.

Along with becoming a magnet for guests, the kitchen has turned into the nerve center of the family.

Opposite: The barriers between today's kitchen and associated rooms, such as the dining and living areas, have virtually disappeared. Instead of resulting in a cold open space, the opposite has occurred. Designers tend to "warm up" the work area by using rich woods, such as maple, for cabinetry and flooring. For a touch of elegance, they often specify marble countertops that contrast with professional-style appliances. Employing similarly styled chairs at the kitchen island and the dining table is an effective way of tying the different spaces together.

Above: The number of features that can be packed into a single work island is truly amazing. This one contains a cooktop, complete with a commercial-style hood overhead; a marble surface ideal for baking; and a host of storage compartments, including ones for produce that needs to be kept in a cool, dark place. A carved-out area gives people perched on the stools a comfortable place to put their legs.

These aren't the only reasons we remodel, however. You may be surprised to learn that more than half the kitchens renovated each year are perfectly functional. In these cases, homeowners are replacing out-of-style components: flooring, faucets, appliances, countertops, and cabinetry. For example, there is a strong trend toward installing cabinets made of maple rather than oak, the traditional standard. Granite, limestone, and soapstone—not to mention concrete—have emerged as popular choices for countertops in more expensive renovations.

Upgrading the kitchen is a sound idea for many of us. Because everyone seems to congregate in the kitchen anyway, it has become the visitors' center of the home. Increasingly, it's where we dine or arrange a buffet supper. Along with becoming a magnet for guests, the kitchen has turned into the nerve center of the family. It is where we put grocery lists, phone messages, and reminders of things to do.

Decades ago, designers recognized the importance of kitchens in family life and began organizing them in a systematic manner. From that process evolved the kitchen floor plans with which we are familiar today: galley, U-shape, and L-shape, among others—with or without a center island.

Since then, kitchen design has undergone a revolution in innovation. For example, the trendsetters who first placed a small butcher-block table in the center of the room probably had no idea how big this device would become in both size and importance. Now known as a work island, this central counter area often includes a drop-in range, an extra sink, a second dishwasher, and supplemental storage.

Other changes to the kitchen have been fueled by changes in the way we live. Both new and remodeled kitchens are being equipped with two work areas containing enough space for two or more people to prepare food, cook, and clean up at the same time. Dual work areas are a tremendous convenience for contemporary households in which both adults share cooking chores. Meals in these homes are pitch-in-and-help projects undertaken by whoever is available, often resulting in more than one cook in the kitchen. With home entertaining at an all-time high in popularity, a kitchen that can accommodate more than one cook is a blessing. If you throw catered parties, dual work areas are practically a necessity.

Much has been written about the needs of empty-nest households and their influence on home design. People whose children have grown up and left home typically scale down by buying or building a residence that better meets their diminished need for space. Yet they still need room to host occasional visits by children and grandchildren, plus space to entertain.

The solution is a kitchen that "expands" to accommodate a large group and "shrinks" for everyday living. To achieve this flexibility, designers tuck a supplemental sink, a second dishwasher, and/or an extra refrigerator in a separate pantry. They are also rediscovering the old-fashioned butler's pantry, which can be filled with additional fixtures and appliances.

Designers and manufacturers are focusing on making kitchens more accessible to people of any age, size, and fitness level. This is no minor issue, considering that the percentage of Americans older than sixty-five has grown from

Right: Who says that too many chefs spoil the soup? Today, meal preparation is often a team effort. This kitchen can accommodate at least three cooks, thanks to its two islands, dual sinks, and a vast amount of streamlined counter space. And this flexibility does not come at the expense of aesthetics. Indeed, much attention has been paid to decorative aspects. For instance, the refrigerator and dishwasher have been fitted with panels that match the surrounding cabinetry, thereby integrating these amenities into the overall look of the room.

Left and right: Thoughtful details, such as a single-lever faucet for the sink and counters that are at a comfortable height, can facilitate cooking chores for everyone. An added bonus of this island's low work surface is that it is hidden from sight by the breakfast bar. Thus, people in the adjacent areas are not exposed to unattractive views of kitchen clutter. And having a kitchen open onto an eating area makes serving easier. Notice how the green wicker chairs pick up the color of the kitchen cabinetry as well as the leaves on the trees outside.

one in every twenty-five in 1900 to one in eight, according to a recent census. There are also many people who have suffered from illnesses or been in accidents that have restricted their physical capabilities.

The movement toward more user-friendly kitchens has been dubbed "universal design." The adjustment may be as subtle as incorporating a single-lever faucet that a person with limited mobility or strength can use easily. Or universal-design principles can be employed throughout a kitchen, appearing in the form of lower countertops, wider aisles, and cabinets that move up and down so that a person in a wheelchair can more easily reach the contents. Also of great help are new appliances—including dishwashers, clothes washers, and dryers—that are fitted with larger, easy-to-read touch pads and visual displays.

Weaving universal-design principles and products into a house before it is built is simple and relatively inexpensive. Bringing universal design into an existing kitchen, however, is expensive, but the cost may be worth it if the planned renovation is extensive.

An integral part of universal design involves rethinking the placement of kitchen appliances in order to reduce physical exertion. Toward that end, situating the dishwasher

eight inches (20cm) above the floor will minimize bending. Though convenient for anyone, an elevated dishwasher could become a necessity at some point down the road.

Considering the many changes in everyday life that have occurred in recent years, it's no wonder that owners of older homes have kitchens that are more woeful than wonderful. It's not unusual for an older kitchen to be plagued with a bad layout, a cramped work area, a lack of counter space, and a dearth of storage. Some kitchen layouts require people to walk through the work triangle—which consists of the sink, range, and refrigerator—thereby disrupting the cook. The work area often is too small to accommodate a dishwasher, a microwave oven, and other desirable appliances that were developed after the home was built. Even a seemingly small inconvenience, such as a lack of counter space on both sides of the stove, can cause big problems: this setup results in the handles of pots and pans hanging over the sides of the range, which places these hot items and their scalding contents within reach of inquisitive young children.

Below: As they are remodeled, older kitchens are being revamped to include multiple workstations, large double-door refrigerators, and commercially inspired appliances. This kitchen even boasts the luxury of a fireplace. **Right:** A thoroughly modern kitchen need not look contemporary. This accommodating kitchen, part of an addition, has been designed to function as the heart of the home—a place where family members can gravitate and enjoy one another's company. It not only boasts the latest in kitchen amenities, but exudes a welcoming atmosphere, thanks to the use of unfitted cherry cabinets, which look more like furnishings one would find in a living room or bedroom. The style of the space reflects the owners' penchant for Arts and Crafts design.

Opposite: With its high ceiling, country decor, and soothing nature-inspired palette, this kitchen encourages whiling away the hours. An eating alcove lined with windows and outfitted with comfortable seating is an additional draw. While the well-placed island invites visiting with the cook, it also forms a barrier that discourages people from walking through the work area and disrupting meal preparation. **Above:** A closer look at this highly efficient kitchen reveals many of the latest trends in kitchen design. The space is filled with commercial-style appliances, including a large restaurant-inspired range, hood, and refrigerator. The modern layout places the sink and range along the same wall, while the refrigerator, used less often, is set off to the side. A gooseneck faucet makes it easier to fill large pots with water, and fixtures mounted underneath the cabinets provide direct illumination for cooking-related tasks.

The keys to making older kitchens function like new are improving the work flow and opening up the space. Placing the sink and range along the same wall does away with traffic between the two. To enlarge kitchens in existing homes, designers are incorporating small, underutilized adjacent spaces, such as a breakfast area, mudroom, or laundry room. Building an addition provides even more space.

Kitchen remodeling goes way beyond space planning, though. Today's appliances are far more varied than those of only a few years ago. Plus, the commercial look has migrated from restaurants into the home. Genuine commercial appliances need large gas lines, special ventilation, and additional structural support, but manufacturers have made modifications to eliminate these requirements for home use and have scaled these devices down so that they work with residential cabinetry.

Dishwashers are quieter than ever and come equipped with an assortment of options and rack designs. Homeowners can choose refrigerators from a wide variety of sizes and configurations, including side-by-side and bottom-freezer models. For those who prefer a more furnished look in the kitchen, there are even refrigerators designed to blend in with cabinetry to create a streamlined effect. Retro designs are available for appliances as well. For instance, a technologically modern range can be styled to resemble an old-fashioned cookstove to set the desired mood.

Sinks are getting bigger, with some divided into double and triple bowls. The sink, in fact, is probably the biggest beneficiary of the resurgence in everything stainless steel, a revival spawned by the recent popularity of the commercial look. Not only has the sink gained a fresh appearance, but it has become more durable and easy to clean. Stainless steel has become quite fashionable for counters, too.

The institutional flavor so prevalent today has also spurred design interest in gooseneck faucets. While these fixtures have an intriguing silhouette, they are also highly practical, facilitating the cleaning of large pots.

A converse trend to incorporating the utilitarian look is upgrading the kitchen with a more luxurious appearance. In fact, some fixture manufacturers have achieved a first: gleaming brass fixtures that are sturdy enough to stand up to abrasive cleaners.

Solid-surfacing has emerged as a classic choice for countertops. This man-made material, produced under a number of brand names, is durable, easy to maintain, and available in a wide variety of colors and textures to blend with any kitchen's palette. Easy to clean and economical, plastic laminate is another option that is available in an ever-growing selection of colors and stain-hiding patterns. Ceramic tile is extremely durable, while butcher block and marble remain favorites of bakers.

The latest practice among serious cooks is to call upon a mix of several countertop materials. If you like plastic laminate, choose it as the primary counter material. Employ ceramic tile on counters flanking the range to handle hot pots, then use butcher block and marble in the baking area for kneading dough and making confections, respectively.

Since every smidgen of space in the kitchen counts, it comes as no surprise that storage is receiving special attention from cabinet manufacturers and designers. Appliance garages, lazy Susans, recycling centers, and various configurations of drawers and cubbyholes offer specialized kitchen storage. And homeowners are putting in more cabinetry as they remodel. The dead space that once was particularly noticeable above upper cabinetry is disappearing as designers install units to the ceiling.

With the desire to make the most of precious space, inventive manufacturers, designers, and homeowners have devised numerous clever storage ideas. For example, there are holders for cookbooks and other items that are designed to be mounted beneath upper cabinets and pulled down when needed. A narrow shelf that takes up little room can be installed to hold spices and other small items used every day. Many home decorators follow the example of commercial

Above: Solid-surfacing, a favorite for countertops, is equally suitable as a desktop—especially in the kitchen where it blends seamlessly with the work counters. Glass-front cabinetry not only puts colorful dishware on display but also makes finding items easier. **Below:** A small kitchen can benefit from specialized storage, such as dividers for cookie sheets, tall platters, and other serving pieces, as well as pullout shelves for baking tins and dishes. Hanging storage for pots and pans keeps them right at hand. **Opposite, bottom, left:** This highly organized drawer contains four separate compartments, used to keep everything from recycling to dog food tidily out of the way. **Opposite, bottom, right:** There's no need to feel harried or hassled in the kitchen. Prowling through cabinets for the right pan is a thing of the past in a kitchen with open metal shelving directly beneath the cooktop.

Above: In many contemporary kitchens, multiple counters provide plenty of work space for more than one person. But there's no need to employ the same material for all of the surfaces. In fact, the use of different materials can increase the efficiency of a kitchen. While most of the counter space along the back wall in this kitchen has a plastic laminate surface that looks like wood, the small counters flanking the stove are topped with ceramic tile to accommodate hot pots and pans.

kitchens by adding a hanging storage system that attaches to the backsplash for ladles and such.

Homeowners are requesting lighting mounted under the cabinets to brighten work counters. When it comes to overall illumination, there is a large demand for recessed ceiling fixtures controlled with rheostats. These elements are just part of the great increase in electrical wiring that has made its way into the kitchen to handle additional appliances, television sets, VCRs, stereo speakers, and computers.

Replacing the floor is yet another route to a fresh kitchen demeanor. It is easy to lay down vinyl tiles, which can be combined to create interesting patterns. Wood, sealed for protection against spills and stains, is becoming more and more popular for kitchen floors. A relatively new entry among flooring options is laminate flooring, which comes in varieties that simulate the look of wood and other materials. Laying down a laminate floor can be an excellent do-it-yourself project. In most cases, this type of floor can be installed over the flooring already in place. Incorporating ceramic tile, however, is not a project to undertake on your own. While it's more expensive, ceramic tile may well be worth the cost if you choose one of the new slip-resistant finishes, combining safety with good looks.

Happily, there's no need to completely renovate your kitchen to give it a new personality. Repainting the kitchen in a different color scheme creates the biggest visual impact for your money and time, requiring perhaps only a weekend's worth of labor. If that seems like too much effort, limit your brushwork to the cabinets, or remove doors from some of the upper cabinets and paint the interior so that it complements the overall color scheme.

As you redesign and redecorate, remember that in today's kitchen, the rule—not the exception—is a blissful marriage of form and function. Thanks to new products that both cater to the way we operate and contribute decorative style, kitchens are working and looking better than ever before.

As you redesign and redecorate, remember that in today's kitchen, the rule—not the exception—is a blissful marriage of form and function.

Above: Homeowners often incorporate a television into the kitchen so that they can catch the news or, in many cases, cooking shows. A corner cabinet not only makes a space-efficient home for this amenity, but also offers a better angle for viewing. This pleasant kitchen gives occupants a generous amount of natural light, thanks to a picture window and a skylight. Track lighting steps in to provide additional illumination. **Opposite:** Wood flooring has gained great popularity in the kitchen, as it can now be sealed effectively against damage from spills. Small rugs can be placed in areas where one tends to stand for extended periods of time, such as in front of the sink, to provide extra cushioning underfoot.

CHAPTER FIVE

WORKING

Perhaps nothing better illustrates the current demand for residences to accommodate several activities at once than the growing popularity of working at home. While home has always been where parents planned budgets and children wrestled with schoolwork, until recently, there was no specific area designed to accommodate these tasks. Instead, such activities generally were undertaken in the middle of the dining room table. As a result, at mealtime, materials had to be packed up and moved. Moreover, messy activities, such as arts and crafts projects, threatened to damage fine woods and finishes.

The trend to create specialized areas within the same room caught up with working at home in the early 1980s. Nowadays, many new homes are fitted with office space in the kitchen for paying bills, planning events, and doing homework, and older homes are being remodeled to include a similar amenity.

Homework and bill paying are probably the most common forms of working at home. For these, an office in the kitchen is eminently suitable. All that's needed is a desk surface for writing or word processing. It's best to have a little bit of distance between the meal preparation area and the desk setup so that the different activities can take place comfortably at the same time. Plus, you don't want food crumbs or spilled milk ending up on paperwork or the computer. Desirable extras include shelving for dictionaries and other reference books, as well as compartments for such small items as bank statements, bills, and checkbooks. You can even incorporate kitchen cabinetry that includes file drawers.

In the kitchen office setup, children can study after school and after dinner. When the kids have gone to bed, mom or dad can use the space to update the family finances, compile the guest list for a weekend cookout, or surf the Internet.

Nowadays, many new homes are fitted with office space in the kitchen for paying bills, planning events, and doing homework.

Pages 78–79: An office in a master suite is a quiet setting away from the hubbub. During the day, especially, such an office offers a calm and visually appealing environment in which to work. This built-in arrangement features lights mounted beneath the shelves, directly above the desk, so that one person can work late into the night without disturbing a sleeping partner. Situating the desk area a good distance away from the bed also facilitates this goal. **Opposite:** Outfitted with a desk and a comfortable chair, the kitchen becomes a great place to pay bills or plan menus as water boils. And, for families with young children, it's a spot where the kids can color or do schoolwork under the watchful eye of a parent fixing dinner. This desk, which matches the kitchen cabinetry, has file cabinets, a corkboard for pinning messages and lists of things to do, and special slots for books. The rich, deep hue of the wood is reminiscent of a library. **Right:** To achieve the least amount of disruption, this home office is located safely out of the way of the main kitchen work zone. Though compact, the arrangement easily accommodates both a computer and space for laying out papers. A shelf with dividers is used for sorting bills, while the cabinetry above, which contains both open and concealed storage, is employed for kitchen-associated items.

If working in the kitchen puts you too close to the temptations of snacks and sweets, there are plenty of other places where you can set up an office. One is the master suite. The advantage to this secluded location is that it affords extra privacy and quiet. The drawback is that it may be inconvenient for one person to work late into the night if the other wants to go to bed.

If you find that a work area in the master suite suits your purposes, a comfortable armchair and desk may be all you need. It's best in this case for the children to have a separate work area, which usually can be set up in their bedrooms or in a space they share.

For the most part, the living room or family room lacks sufficient privacy to function as a home office. Accomplishing work chores is difficult in an area where people tend to congregate and talk, watch television, and listen to the stereo. Even if no one uses the space at the time you would need it, home-entertainment equipment presents powerful distractions.

However, if you have no choice but to set up shop in the living or family room, there are measures you can take to carve out as effective a work environment as possible. One such step is to separate the work area from the rest of the room by putting up a tall folding screen. This strategy creates a dedicated work space that you can furnish with a desk, a chair, and a filing cabinet. The advantage to this approach is that you can leave an unfinished project as is without disrupting anyone else's activities or causing the rest of the room to look messy. The screen also blocks the view to the television and any other visual distractions in the main part of the room. Stylish folding screens are available at home-furnishings stores

Left: If your only option is to incorporate a home office into the main living area, minimize its intrusion by blending it into a wall of cabinetry. In a wise use of space, the cabinetry pictured here has been situated directly beneath a second-story landing. While the unit features display shelves filled with family photographs and objets d'art to enhance the living area, it also comfortably houses two work surfaces—both of which are closed off with cabinet doors to hide clutter. **Above:** In this traditionally styled work space, cabinet doors conceal computer components and trays for "works in progress," while glass doors keep reference books within easy sight but dust-free. Shelves located just above the work surface are filled with a favorite collection that provides a personal note.

and can be purchased quite inexpensively—a great solution for adding a whole new work space.

Other areas where you can carve out space for a home office include a stair landing and a wide hallway. That front entrance hall that no one uses can be the perfect spot to set up a work space that will remain relatively undisturbed. One strategy that has enjoyed immense popularity is the fashioning of an office area out of a wide and shallow hallway closet. A thick board for a desk surface and overhead shelving can be installed as a weekend project by a do-it-yourself woodworker. This type of office can easily be converted back into a closet later. The obvious drawback is a loss of storage space, which, depending on your needs, may be more important than having a home workstation.

People who conduct more than family or personal business at home usually require a more elaborate and permanent setup. Along with a computer, you may need a separate phone, an answering machine, a fax, and even a copier or scanner. A home that already includes a separate study boasts an obvious spot for an office. Lacking that, however, the attic,

Opposite: A wide hallway, a common feature in contemporary houses, is an excellent setting for a home office, especially for someone who works late in the evening. After other family members have gone to bed, the hallway is entirely private. **Below, left:** Space beneath the stairs, often wasted in homes, can be put to good use as extra storage or as a work area. If you try a setup like this, you may want to take various space-saving measures, such as mounting a phone, light fixtures, and shelving on the wall to free up precious desk space. **Below, right:** When space is at a premium, you need to be resourceful. Here, the area underneath the stairs has been fitted with custom-made drawers that hold supplies and office equipment.

a loft, or the basement may provide the amount of space you need. An advantage to these locations is that they are conveniently removed from everyday household activities and traffic patterns, making them great places in which to concentrate and bask in privacy. If you are fortunate enough to have a spare bedroom, that space presents another option. It can double as a guest room if you include a bed and a nightstand or even a sleeper sofa and an end table.

Before you buy any equipment, make scale drawings of your ideal home office on paper. This avoids the trouble of moving bookcases and other bulky items if your original plan for the layout turns out to be impractical. Note the number and location of electrical outlets. You may want to call in an electrician to install more.

Experience has shown that L- and U-shaped work areas are the most efficient. These layouts ensure that everything you need is close at hand. A turn of your chair to the left or right puts you at the computer keyboard, fax machine, or filing cabinets. Desks can be purchased in these configurations or created with mix-and-match components. Positioning one leg of the work setup so that it juts out from a wall will emphasize the separation between the office area and the rest of the room in a multipurpose space.

But suppose you require a home office setup that includes work space for two? In more and more dual-income households, both adults discover that they need their own work areas. While the best way of achieving privacy and quiet for deep concentration is to create separate offices, your home may lack the space for such an arrangement.

If your only option is to double up, dedicate a room, such as a spare bedroom, to working at home. Carve the space into two work areas, each with its own work surface and chair. Make sure that both occupants have places for pencils, a ruler, and other necessary supplies, as this small measure will eliminate the need to continually get up and walk across the room. Separate computers are desirable if you have the space, but try to make do with one printer.

People who conduct more than family or personal business at home usually require a more elaborate and permanent setup.

Above and opposite: If you do all your work out of your home, you are likely to need a secluded setup where you can be free of distractions and hold business meetings. Building an addition, such as the one on the right side of this house, is an effective way of fulfilling such a need. The home office is a comfortable distance away from the heart of family activities and has a separate entrance so that clients don't need to walk through the residence. Dark wood paneling and a coffered ceiling set a traditional tone.

The optimal configuration entails placing the work areas so that they face away from each other. This type of layout will create at least a feeling of solitude. It also reduces the tendency to be distracted by what the other person is doing, as well as the temptation to talk about other matters instead of getting your work finished. Place filing cabinets and other storage items in a closet if possible to keep clutter in the room to a minimum.

In tailoring your personal work space, bear in mind the guidelines that designers follow. The best height for a typing surface is twenty-six inches (66cm), while the optimal height for other work surfaces is thirty inches (76cm). A lighting scheme that incorporates a combination of direct and ambient fixtures reduces eye strain, and the computer should receive indirect illumination to avoid glare. Take advantage of carpeting to muffle noise. If that's not possible, a strategically placed tall unit—a bookcase, for example—will help deflect distracting sounds.

Don't forget to give yourself a treat. One of the best features you can include is something on which to focus when you are thinking, either silently or aloud. Positioning the desk so that you can take advantage of an outdoor view will not only bring pleasure but will also provide a refreshing break for your eyes. Another way to go is to hang a favorite piece of artwork above your desk.

With more people working at home these days, furniture options abound. You can buy desks, chairs, file cabinets, and bookcases in virtually any style from furniture stores. Some furniture companies manufacture a complete home office literally in a box. This office-in-an-armoire is ideal for a multifunctional room, as it enables you to conceal the contents from view simply by closing the doors when you finish your tasks. Thus, the look and mood of the rest of the room are not compromised. Some of these office setups are sold in kits that you assemble.

A more permanent solution is outfitting an office with kitchen cabinetry. Not only can kitchen base cabinets be

Opposite, top: An L-shaped configuration such as this allows two people to work comfortably side by side while giving each a sense of personal space. Flush against the wall, the setup sports a streamlined look and takes advantage of a row of generously sized windows. A plump armchair gives occupants a break from their desks and offers a comfy spot for reading.

Opposite, bottom: Home offices take many forms—from a strictly business design to a denlike setting furnished with a tavern table as a desk and a comfortable wing chair for guests. If your preference is for a cozy home office, why not eschew track lighting for a chandelier and tuck the computer away in an old-fashioned-looking armoire? Instead of sterile file cabinets, use small boxes to hold business papers.

Right: A back porch has been enclosed and transformed into an inviting home office that receives lots of natural light. So as not to obstruct the view provided by a bank of windows, all storage has been placed underneath the countertop, which curves outward at one point to create a comfortable desk area. Translucent shades allow light to pour into the room yet preserve privacy.

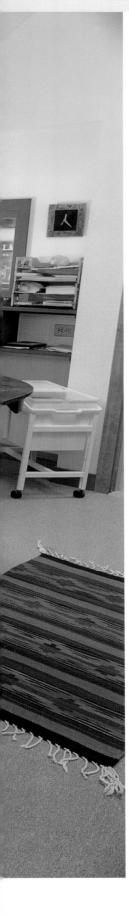

Left: Tucked under the eaves, a home office is shared by a husband and wife, an engineer and a sculptor, respectively. The couple's former dining table serves as a divider between the two work areas while also providing a place to spread out papers and blueprints. Another inventive feature is the aqua desktop, fashioned from a painted door. Each person has a computer, both of which are hooked up to the same printer— a strategy that saves both money and space. **Above:** A close look at the sculptor's work area reveals that it is fully equipped for business endeavors. An interior window, painted the same bright shade as the large desktop, livens up the corner and opens it up a bit. The occupant "commutes" between this space and the art studio located downstairs.

fitted with drawers to hold files, as mentioned earlier, but they can also be designed to accommodate desktops. And kitchen cabinetry is no longer restricted to the kitchen. In fact, the installation of these cabinets in home offices outside the kitchen follows the trend of incorporating this type of storage into other areas, such as the family room, where cabinets are used to house media equipment. In the home office, upper cabinets become tailored bookshelves instead of storage space for dinnerware. While opting for kitchen cabinets may entail more of a commitment than other arrangements, a big advantage is that they are available in a variety of decorative styles and materials suitable for virtually any budget.

To save space, choose home office equipment that can do double duty, such as a fax machine that also functions as a copier or incorporates a telephone and answering machine. Other space-saving ideas include purchasing a telephone and light fixtures that can be attached to the wall rather than taking up desk space. You might also want to incorporate a desk with a leaf that can be pulled out to expand the work surface. Virtually everyone knows that computer keyboards can be housed in a retractable shelf below the work surface, but you also can conceal a computer printer in a desk drawer to free up considerable space on top.

Now's the time to be inventive with storage. Large items—bolts of fabric, floor plans, or mailing tubes—can easily be kept in inexpensive woven baskets set on the floor or hidden behind a decorative screen. Another way to express your creativity is with accessories. There are no company guidelines to follow, so you are free to decorate a home office any way you choose. Instead of a framed diploma, why not display souvenirs of your travels or items you collect?

Endeavors that include meeting with clients in an at-home office usually require a separate entrance, as it's awkward for a business client to walk through a family's living space. Having a direct entry into the office also frees the household from keeping the in-between areas organized at all times and allows family members to retain their privacy.

CHAPTER SIX

DREAMING

When the chores of the day are finally done, it's time for some rest and relaxation. More and more, the setting of choice is the master suite, the most intimate space of the home. We treat this area as a treasured haven, a place where we can escape all the chaos of the world outside.

The master suite has evolved far beyond what it was only a few years back. In the 1940s, for example, the largest bedroom, which wasn't much bigger than the others, was reserved for the head of the family. By the 1950s, architects and builders were beginning to include a half- or three-quarter-bath that consisted of a water closet, sink, and shower unit. The concept proved so popular with homeowners that it wasn't long before the master suite became a focus of consumer attention and builder marketing, quickly growing in terms of both size and features.

Today, the master suite is a place to unwind and pamper yourself in privacy. Typically, it is composed of a bedroom with a separate bath and a dressing area. Many suites also incorporate a sitting area, which can take the form of an airy, light-filled sunroom. Other arrangements include a wet bar with a refrigerator, a separate study or adjoining home office, or a private terrace or deck.

Many homes built before the 1960s lack a master suite. If your abode is missing this type of bedroom retreat, go ahead and create one! In a home that has more than one

Pages 92–93: This master suite caters to its occupants with soaring windows that usher in natural light and a sitting area outfitted with a full-size sofa. Pillows are strewn lavishly across both the couch and bed, offering the utmost in comfort. Country-style furnishings infuse the space with a relaxed feel, while sconces with candles add a hint of romance.

Above: A true refuge, the master suite has grown into a space that is more like a private apartment than a mere bedroom. Here, a chaise beckons residents to recline by the fire, while an upholstered armchair situated by the window invites reading. Architectural features, including columns and a vaulted ceiling, deftly zone space, enhancing the sense of sumptuousness. **Opposite:** A bedroom sitting area does not need to be elaborate. In fact, it can be as simple as a pair of comfortable chairs positioned at the foot of the bed. A table between them provides a place to set that morning cup of coffee and display treasured heirlooms.

We treat this area as a treasured haven,

a place where we can escape all the chaos of the world outside.

Opposite: This bedroom comes complete with the offerings of a spa. Providing the ultimate in relaxation, it includes a whirlpool bath nestled into a windowed alcove—the perfect place to unwind after a long day. **Above:** A favorite amenity in the master suite is a sitting area designed like a sunroom. In this example, wraparound windows flank glazed doors that open onto a balcony. **Left:** Many master suites include a separate dressing area with built-in storage containing cubbies and drawers for sweaters, hats, and shoes, as well as large closets for long garments. Built-in storage is a smart way to go, as the dressing room tends to be a relatively small space.

bath, the easiest strategy is to combine a hall bath and the largest adjacent bedroom by breaking through their common wall. This approach may require you to sacrifice storage space if the wall contains closets. Incorporating new closets is one way to retrieve some of what was lost. An armoire or another freestanding unit can also be called upon to pitch in and pick up any slack.

Does your bedroom have the luxury of a larger-than-necessary closet? It may be big enough to rework into both a storage and dressing area. Closet organizers and systems can help consolidate storage space significantly, creating sufficient room to change clothes or, with the addition of a vanity, apply makeup (just make sure you incorporate good lighting).

If combining spaces isn't an option, increase the room you have with an addition. More and more, families are adding a master bath and, in many instances, a dressing area, thereby converting a humdrum bedroom into a dream getaway. Besides enhancing your daily life, adding a bath—according to current statistics—is one of the surest ways to increase the value of your home when you're in the market to sell.

Even a home with a fully functional master suite can be improved. Adding a terrace off the bedroom enables you to enjoy morning coffee—or a nightcap—in privacy. This intimate outdoor space might even substitute as an open-air office on pleasant days. An additional advantage to opening the room up to the outdoors is that doing so encourages natural light to enter and frames views that make the space seem bigger.

For many people, exercise is becoming an increasingly important part of the daily routine. Instead of spending money on a gym membership, invest it to create a workout area that you can use whenever you wish—and with no one watching you. A home workout setup also eliminates the obstacle of actually having to travel to the gym—there's no excuse not to exercise when everything you need is right in front of you.

Store weights and other equipment beneath the bed and undertake your routine in the sitting area. To create a sitting area where none exists, expand the master bedroom with an addition. Many homeowners are adding on a sunroom and furnishing it with charming wicker chairs and tables. Besides creating room to exercise, this strategy provides a comfortable area with a pleasant outdoor ambience in which to relax after work.

Many of the influences that have prevailed in master suites are also evident in other bedrooms. A good example is the trend in new upscale housing to allocate a bath for each bedroom, in effect creating a series of mini-suites for children and guests as well as the owners. Children's rooms often include individual study spaces and a common area for rainy-day activities. Some kids' rooms are also set up to share a bathroom that has a common tub and shower area but individual water closets. Other children's rooms may have a joint outdoor deck. Many guest rooms are being designed to include a desk or some other type of work area in which a computer can be set up easily.

While kids' rooms and guest rooms are acquiring many of the amenities of master suites, they continue to have some very different requirements. Children's rooms, for instance, need sturdy, easy-clean surfaces and lots of storage space to house toys and school materials. In the guest room, on the other hand, storage space is secondary to welcoming details, such as a shelf for current magazines and best-sellers, a comfortable reading chair, and perhaps throw pillows. You might also want to include such warm touches as an aromatic candle or a vase filled with flowers.

Regardless of the type, bedrooms are indeed for more than just sleeping. They are called upon for dressing and

Children's rooms need sturdy, easy-clean surfaces and lots of storage space to house toys and school materials.

Left: Many children's rooms take the form of small suites. Not only is this bedroom stocked with an abundance of storage—namely two freestanding cupboards and a low bookshelf that fits perfectly under a window—but it also has a wicker chair and even a small sofa for hosting visitors. The former doubles as a valet, while the latter folds out into a bed for sleep-overs. **Below, left:** When space is limited, children's furniture that combines accommodations for sleeping, storage, and doing homework is a welcome feature. This bunk bed has been designed so that an accompanying desk and dresser fit effortlessly underneath it. **Below, right:** Manufacturers of children's furniture offer pieces that are specifically designed to accommodate a computer as well as provide enough space for papers. These modular pieces take advantage of what is often wasted space—a corner. A window sheds light on homework.

grooming as well as working, studying, entertaining children, exercising, and watching television. As a result, space planning is crucial for comfort and practicality.

The largest item in a bedroom is, not surprisingly, the bed. Whether it's a traditional four-poster or a contemporary platform sort, it determines the decorative style of the entire room. Sizes range from twin to California king. Choose the one that will both provide the most comfort and fit in well with the amount of space that you have.

Traditionally, the bed is placed in the center of the wall opposite the doorway into the room. But this arrangement is not cast in stone. Other common approaches involve placing the bed against the same wall as the door, nestling it into the embrace of a corner, or angling it out from a corner. If there's space, you may even want to situate the bed in the middle of the room.

Almost as important as the bed itself is the matter of bed linens. Bearing in mind that people spend, on average, one-third of their lives asleep, you should select sheets and coverings that best combine quality and comfort, taking into account the need for warmth and noting allergies. Rotate bedding on a seasonal basis to redecorate. Lightweight, pale-color linens are great for summer, while darker, heavier ones inject a sense of coziness in winter.

Since, more and more, we are looking to bedrooms as personal retreats, it is important to make them not only comfortable, but visually enticing—they should be places in which we relish spending time. Along that vein, homeowners are refusing to settle for what are often bland, boxy rooms. To add architectural interest, owners are raising ceilings in the cathedral style and applying crown moldings to walls. Flat ceilings are being decorated with medallions and ceiling fans, which help circulate air and thus reduce heating and cooling bills throughout the year. Skylights are yet another way to imbue a bedroom with added appeal. They frame a view of sky and sun that changes with the weather and can be opened for ventilation.

Below: Placed on an angle in the center of the room, the bed is the focal point of this space. The arrangement also makes the most of a fireplace, allowing occupants to read in bed while basking in the glow of the flames. Thanks to the river-rock surround, an abundance of pale wood, and a dried vine wrapped around one of the bedposts, the room has the air of a natural retreat.

Opposite: The bed in this peaceful bedroom has a more traditional placement—centered against the wall opposite the doorway. The four-poster style and the plethora of pillows lend this basic feature a sense of majesty. On either side, nightstands support matching lamps, while a desk off to the left provides a quiet spot for the "old-fashioned" art of letter writing.

To add architectural interest, owners are raising ceilings in the cathedral style and applying crown moldings to walls.

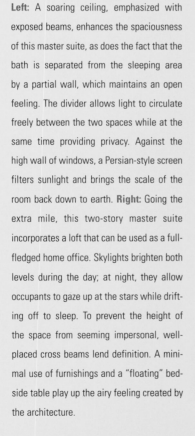

Left: A soaring ceiling, emphasized with exposed beams, enhances the spaciousness of this master suite, as does the fact that the bath is separated from the sleeping area by a partial wall, which maintains an open feeling. The divider allows light to circulate freely between the two spaces while at the same time providing privacy. Against the high wall of windows, a Persian-style screen filters sunlight and brings the scale of the room back down to earth. **Right:** Going the extra mile, this two-story master suite incorporates a loft that can be used as a full-fledged home office. Skylights brighten both levels during the day; at night, they allow occupants to gaze up at the stars while drifting off to sleep. To prevent the height of the space from seeming impersonal, well-placed cross beams lend definition. A minimal use of furnishings and a "floating" bedside table play up the airy feeling created by the architecture.

Opposite: Today's master suites are incorporating more and more glazing. And imaginative architects are combining elements of different eras. Here, modern casements are topped off with a traditional half-moon shape. Notice how the lines of this crowning feature are echoed by the curved woodwork in the corners of the room. **Above:** The new trend in window seats is the incorporation of drawers that pull out instead of hinged tops that require the seat pad to be removed to open the unit. **Left:** Displaying an ingenious use of space, this compact dressing area contains a built-in table, two columns of drawers, and a large mirror. Best of all, it can be closed off at a moment's notice thanks to a set of double doors. The same wood is carried over to the adjacent window seat, which features easy-access drawers and gives occupants a place to stretch out in the sun.

Overscale windows, often enlivened with half-round top elements, and dramatic drapery treatments are high on homeowners' wish lists. Perhaps fueled by the desire for a custom look, window treatments are again becoming multi-layered with the addition of sheers accompanied by other decorative flourishes, such as shirring and elaborate tiebacks. The trend toward emphasizing windows has spilled over into drapery hardware, which has become a decorative element in itself. Curtain rods come in a range of materials. Metal ones, for instance, are available in a variety of exotic finishes, from flat to luminescent.

Built-in storage has proven to be decorative as well as practical in bedrooms. Wall cabinetry can house the television set as well as other media equipment, office files, books, children's toys, and display objects. Some homeowners prefer that the units remain open to view, while others conceal the contents behind closed doors. A mixture of both types of storage is available, too.

An always popular idea is a window seat. Besides providing a prime relaxation spot and affording plenty of natural light for curling up with a book, this feature offers extra storage space. While the classic window seat opens from the top with a hinged lid, this approach is inconvenient. It requires removing the seat cushion and propping up the lid while digging through the contents. Invariably, you find yourself bent over, rummaging around with one hand and holding the top up with the other. Fortunately, there's a simple way to avoid this awkwardness: ask your carpenter to incorporate drawers instead of a hinged lid into the design. Then, when you need to store or retrieve an item, both hands are free to sort through the contents.

Window seats are superbly suited for traditional decorating schemes and window treatments. Upholstering the cushion in a pattern that embodies historic designs furthers the theme, as does embellishing the front of the seat with decorative molding.

Contemporary schemes are particularly suited for built-in storage. For example, interior designers and architects will fashion a wall and the headboard of a bed into one sleek unit. In some cases, the configuration also includes nightstands and shelves for books. Some arrangements even include an overhang that extends from the wall to house recessed lighting fixtures for bedtime reading. Customized controls enable one person to read late into the night while the other sleeps in peace.

Built-ins can also be an economical solution to the problem of insufficient storage. The cost can become part of a building or remodeling budget and paid off slowly over the length of a loan. Thus, you avoid the up-front expense incurred with the purchase of armoires and the like.

Though wall-to-wall carpeting remains the floor treatment of choice for bedrooms, don't pass up an opportunity to add visual warmth by retrofitting these spaces with hardwood planking that can then be topped with large area rugs. A great way to add the look of wood flooring easily is to select a plastic laminate look-alike. Plastic laminate flooring

Above: Windows and sliding glass doors visually enlarge a compact bedroom, while an adjoining balcony physically extends the living space. To maximize the amount of storage without sacrificing valuable natural light, the designer has incorporated a built-in unit that works its way around the glazing. The arrangement features closets, drawers, and a window seat that takes advantage of the view. When the sun goes down, recessed lights directly above the cushioned seat step in. **Left:** In this airy, open space, a wall of storage that "floats" in the center of the room separates the sleeping area from the bath. The multipurpose divider also acts as a headboard, incorporates drawers for clothing, and provides a shelf for keeping bedtime necessities close at hand. Reading lamps mounted on either side allow each occupant to have direct illumination. **Opposite:** Hardwood flooring is becoming increasingly popular in the bedroom, especially when combined with area rugs for a bit of comfort. Here, small rugs are positioned on either side of the room to ease occupants out of bed in the morning. Although the walls are white, the room exudes a tremendous amount of warmth, thanks to the upholstery on the chaise and cheerful bed linens.

Left: Color is a great decorating tool for the rugged individualist. It can even be fashioned into a mural as in this room, which is decorated so that the last thing the young occupant sees before falling asleep is a dog baying at the moon. Motifs of the American West—horseshoe accents on the bed frame, a comforter sporting the look of denim, and bandanna tiebacks on the curtains—establish a definitive sense of style. **Opposite, top:** What young boy wouldn't like his room to resemble a fishing camp in the woods? Both the forest green paint used on the walls and the rustic log bed frame contribute to the wilderness theme. The bunk bed is great for hosting a sleep-over. **Opposite, bottom:** The other side of the bedroom features desk space for studying and working on the computer, shelving for books and collections, and drawers for clothes. Notice how the pine unit and the wall paneling behind it work with the style of the bed.

Decorative paint treatments abound, capable of giving

bedrooms of every sort a personal stamp.

that resembles other stylish materials, such as marble, is also readily available.

Color is a powerful tool for setting the right mood in a bedroom. Cool colors, such as blues and greens, have a tranquil effect, which can transform an ordinary bedroom into a peaceful haven. And decorative paint treatments abound, capable of giving bedrooms of every sort a personal stamp. In the nursery, ragging creates expanses of white clouds and blue skies, resulting in a serene environment. Stencils—clowns and other whimsical figures for young children's rooms, vertical stripes for high school students—are extremely versatile decorating devices. A trompe l'oeil scene is a sophisticated addition to a master bedroom. If creating one seems too daunting a task, paint the molding to look like marble.

In older houses, paint treatments can hide the flaws in walls of less-than-stellar condition. A simple means of disguise is textured paint, which is available at retailers.

Devising decorative paint schemes is a fun do-it-yourself project that everyone in the family can enjoy. Patterns and ideas for colors and different applications abound in craft and decorating magazines. Many of these are easily adaptable to a range of decorating challenges.

Adding dressmaker details is yet another way to bring a personal touch to bedrooms as well as to other spaces within the home. Apply tassels to slipcovers, or line a bed canopy with a fabric that coordinates with the bed dressings. A very simple idea is to purchase a piece of cashmere—or hem a trendy puckered fabric—that you can drape over an upholstered headboard. These kinds of layering devices can be changed periodically to keep the decor visually fresh.

Adding dressmaker details is yet another way
to bring a personal touch to bedrooms as well as
to other spaces within the home.

Left: Small details can have great decorative impact in a bedroom. Ruffled seat cushions, covers on the chair backs, and other thoughtful touches bring homespun charm to this sitting area in a master suite.

Right: To enhance the allure of a bedroom, try incorporating special architectural features, such as beautiful stained glass windows. Here, the owners have made the most of such windows by situating a cushioned wicker chaise beside them, thereby creating a pleasant place to kick back and enjoy the paper or browse through a magazine. A settee at the foot of the bed provides a convenient spot for putting on shoes in the morning.

CHAPTER SEVEN

BATHING

When it comes to bathrooms, we expect more. Gone is the simple family bath of the 1940s and 1950s. Back then, a home had just one bathroom, located off a hallway and consisting of the basics—a tub (sometimes with, sometimes without, a showerhead), a water closet, and a sink. Today, however, there may be many baths in one house, and they are more likely to include a double vanity, a separate shower and tub, and a private enclosure for the water closet.

Over the years, the one-bathroom home disappeared as architects and developers gave the heads of the household their own private bathroom and dressing area, transforming the master bedroom into a master suite. In many cases, the children also got a shared bath, usually inserted between their bedrooms. Even visitors got a bath—a powder room near the entry. Technically a half-bath, the typical powder room consists of a sink and water closet, allowing guests to freshen up after arriving and before leaving.

As is the case with the kitchen, renovating a bathroom is a good investment. In the United States, updating an existing bath returns an average of 77 percent of your investment at resale time according to some studies. An even better investment is the addition of a bathroom, which pays back a whopping 91 percent. In some cases, an addition is an unnecessary indulgence, though not as much of one as you might think; many new luxury homes have a private bath for each bedroom, not to mention his-and-her baths in the master suite.

Affluent baby boomers are leading the way in rehabilitating older baths. In some instances, this practice is labeled by experts as part of a trend to over-renovate homes. Simply put, over-renovating consists of undertaking improvements that are so idiosyncratic or expensive that it's virtually impossible for the owners to recoup their investment at resale. For example, that gas fireplace one homeowner insisted on installing for the no-fuss soothing ambience it would add to the master bath may strike a potential buyer as merely silly.

Over the years, the one-bathroom home disappeared as architects and developers gave the heads of the household their own private bathroom and dressing area, transforming the master bedroom into a master suite.

Pages 112–113: The bath of today's master suite is likely to include a large, jetted tub set beneath a window so that the bather can enjoy the outdoor view. Dual vanities with individual mirrors are a common feature, allowing two people to get ready for a busy day at the same time. **Opposite:** With a whirlpool bath, a separate shower, and an abundance of storage, this master bath leaves little to be desired. A glass partition on the stall allows light to filter into the shower, while a built-in niche provides a convenient spot for shampoo and soap. Towels are easily accessible, thanks to open cubbies in the lower portion of the vanity; extras are stored in a cupboard that fits snugly between the doorway and shower. A liberal use of marble, employed for the floor, countertop, shower, and tub surround, results in a seamless, luxurious look. **Right:** In this bathroom, a partial wall sections off the toilet for privacy; often, this idea is taken a step further by situating the toilet in a completely enclosed area with a door. But bathroom design today does not stop with the functional aspects of the space. The trend is to do away with the utilitarian look and give the bath the same decorative attention as the "living" areas of the home. Here, the effect is achieved with painted beadboard wainscoting, floral wallpaper, a vanity that resembles a freestanding piece of furniture, and an ornate mirror that one might find hanging above a fireplace.

Why would someone over-renovate? Statistically speaking, we live in our houses for about thirteen years, almost twice as long as what was occurring in the 1980s. Well-heeled baby boomers who have settled into their current homes and think of these dwellings as their permanent residences are remodeling to suit themselves rather than the resale market. For everyone else, it's probably a good idea to stick to the accepted guideline of limiting the cost of improvements to the value of the home.

Nowadays, the design spotlight is focused squarely on the master bath. The idea is to promote relaxation and reinvigoration by creating a spalike atmosphere. In both new and remodeled master baths, a large whirlpool tub is the centerpiece of choice. Though we usually associate this therapeutic fixture with sleek contemporary design, it is available in traditional styles. Many owners incorporate large or intricately designed windows, leaded glass panels, and skylights that draw attention to the tub by showering it with light and color. Other owners highlight the whirlpool tub by placing it in an elevated platform or displaying it in a niche, which is sometimes windowed or embellished with an arch. Some even situate the tub near a wall of glass that opens onto a screened garden, thereby creating the sensation of bathing outdoors while retaining privacy. By hanging plants above the tub or placing them on the surrounding ledge, owners complete the transformation of the bath from a purely utilitarian space to one with the ambience of a natural oasis.

The modern master bath incorporates other amenities, such as an overscale clear glass shower stall, a double vanity, and a private water closet. Often, this bath is adjacent to a dressing room as large as a small bedroom.

The separate shower, a welcome amenity when two adults are getting ready for work in the morning or for bed at night, is growing in size and offering more accoutrements. The most common of these features are folding seats, multiple showerheads, and a steam-shower unit. Some master baths even include a sauna.

Opposite: This whirlpool tub is recessed deep into the floor of a secluded niche, affording the bather complete privacy without interfering with the view through the French doors. The lush greenery outside and the potted plants around the edge of the tub create the feeling of bathing in the midst of a garden paradise—an ideal setting for letting one's cares melt away. **Above:** A double vanity is a practical feature for a couple on the go, allowing both people to get ready for work or an evening out at the same time. So that neither party will disrupt the other, each side comes equipped with its own mirrors and drawers. A wraparound mirror allows one to look at oneself from all angles. **Left:** Capitalizing on a garden view, a seamless expanse of glass creates the sensation of bathing or showering outdoors. The enclosure for the overscale shower is also composed of glass, opening up the space and counterbalancing the heaviness of the marble tub surround and back wall. Notice that the greenery outside has been planted to form a leafy barrier that shields occupants from view.

Several years ago, there arose a highly stylish practice of devising custom vanities by inserting basins in antique or reproduction tables and sideboards. Cabinet manufacturers now offer bathroom and kitchen "furniture" pieces in a range of decorative styles. Larger units include soffits with light fixtures and plenty of drawers and shelves. Conventional vanities need not be plain or lacking in style. Many are available with optional moldings and cabinets with glass-front or raised-panel doors.

The double vanity, complete with ample storage space for bath linens and grooming aids, is a big convenience. While most of these have basins at the same height, this need not be the case. A basin placed thirty-six inches (91cm) above the floor accommodates the needs of most adults. But if a family member is taller than average, you can raise the other half of the cabinet so that the second basin is forty-three inches (109cm) off the floor. Thus, both occupants can get ready for work or bed in total comfort.

Below: Seizing upon the trend to fit antique furnishings with sinks, many manufacturers are offering vanities that come ready-made with this effect. The example here boasts an easy-to-maintain surface and handy towel bars on either side. The furnished look is extended by a diminutive marble-topped side table, which can be used for stowing small items. **Right:** This vanity functions as a comfortable dressing table, thanks to a clever design that enables a chair to pull up to it. A freestanding cupboard takes the place of traditional built-in cabinetry and warms up the space.

Opposite: A simple, white pedestal sink and understated old-fashioned sconces fit in with the traditional decor of this bath while counterbalancing its grandeur. A dressing table, complete with a mirror, provides a second spot for grooming. **Above:** A bar located front and center on the vanity keeps towels within easy reach. Filled with clever storage ideas, this bathroom also boasts a built-in hamper, situated just below the open shelving. Mirrors used along two walls make the room appear larger than it really is. **Left:** Vanities that vary in height can make life easier for adults as well as for children. Here, the incorporation of sinks at different levels enables the bathroom to comfortably accommodate siblings—no step stool required. Bold primary colors—appearing in the backsplash, key tiles, towels, and decorative accessories—establish a playful tone, as do the handprints, reminiscent of finger painting, in the basins.

Many design trends and product innovations are appropriate for any type of bath—master, family, or children's. For example, slide-bar units enable a showerhead to be moved up and down a two-foot (61cm) -long vertical bar to accommodate bathers of various heights. Such a showerhead is easily removed from the bar for use as a handheld spray.

To conserve water, low-flush toilets that require a mere 1.6 gallons (6L) of water are now mandated by law in virtually every U.S. jurisdiction. But water conservation is only one aspect of the overhaul of this fixture. Toilets have been restyled for greater design impact and comfort. Some high-end models answer an age-old complaint by offering the luxury of a heated seat.

Today's bath vanities come in a dizzying array of styles, with options of every imaginable sort—tilt-down drawers, slide-out trays, and wire baskets. Countertops are developing along two accepted lines—changes in style and innovations in materials. Along with maple, pecan has gained popularity for upscale bathrooms. While ceramic tile and plastic laminate remain favorite countertop choices, homeowners are also taking advantage of solid-surfacing, which is available in a range of custom colors. Another option in the realm of man-made materials is an integral top, which combines the counter and basin.

Bathroom lighting has changed considerably since the accepted standard was a single-lamp fixture above the sink. Designers now recognize the need for two different types—general and task. General, or ambient, lighting provides uniform illumination throughout the room. Examples of task lighting include ceiling fixtures above the tub, in the shower, and at the vanity. Flanking the mirror with strips of small, bright lamps works well in a contemporary bath for shaving, applying makeup, brushing teeth, and similar chores. A traditionally styled bath looks especially charming when fitted with decorative sconces.

Comfort in the bath is a paramount concern these days. Besides conventional in-the-wall heating units, radiant-floor systems continue to be a popular and effective amenity. So, too, are timer-controlled heat lamps, which make it much easier to step out of a hot shower on a cold day. Heated towel bars, once a luxury item, have come down in cost and are, for many homeowners, an amenity well worth the investment.

The hallway family bath is notoriously small in older houses, with many measuring a mere five by seven feet (1.5 x 2m). However, because of the trend toward having more than one bath, the general hall bath in new homes is often just as cramped. Making the most of a small bath, family or otherwise, requires creative thinking. One solution is to embrace corners when installing bath fixtures. Corner shower units, lavatories, and wall-hung cabinets are readily available in stock materials and conventional sizes. Many of the storage units include a mirror and adjustable shelves, while both corner cabinetry and showers can come with lighting fixtures. Wall-hung cabinetry boasts the advantage of freeing up floor space, thereby increasing the sense of roominess.

To create the illusion of a bigger bath, install a large mirror. Other space-enhancing magic tricks include incorporating a clear glass shower door instead of a textured one, using a uniform finish for fixtures, and establishing a monochromatic color scheme.

If your bathroom window is small, it's time to let in the light. Designers recommend that glazing should equal 10 percent of a bathroom's square footage. Remodeling provides the perfect opportunity to brighten your bath with more—and larger—windows and skylights. Inserting a stained glass panel in front of a bathroom window will not

Opposite, top: If you want the convenience of modern-day innovations but at the same time desire a traditional look, install two pedestal sinks. Here, the old-fashioned theme is enhanced by identical cupboards fitted with lace panels. Providing the utmost privacy, the tub and shower reside in a separate but adjoining room. **Opposite, bottom:** Because there was no room for side-by-side vanities, the owners took advantage of the space on either side of the doorway and installed sinks that fit into the corners of the room. Each area has a wall-mounted light fixture directly overhead and a three-sided mirror that provides views from all angles. **Right:** Long-lasting and easy to clean, ceramic tile remains a favorite material for the bath. Now, however, it is being paired with exotic woods to form interesting combinations. Here, the wood base of the sink warms up the tiles on the counter and surrounding wall space. The vanity is not only eye-catching, but practical as well, packing a lot of storage into a compact space.

Today's bath vanities come in a dizzying array of styles, with options of every imaginable sort—tilt-down drawers, slide-out trays, and wire baskets.

Opposite: The joy of a glass-block enclosure is that it both allows light to filter in and provides privacy. Furthermore, the sense of transparency keeps the bathroom itself looking light and airy. Here, the side of the tub surround has been finished off with a glass-block surface to achieve continuity. **Above:** Like other rooms today, the bath favors skylights and expanses of windows. Such features not only increase the amount of natural light that enters the space, but also bring the beauty of the outdoors inside. With a skylight positioned directly above it, this spalike tub offers the opportunity for a moonlight soak.

only create an intriguing play of light and color, but also ensure privacy if you have nearby neighbors. The actual flow of light within the bath is being given special consideration, too. For example, in many a remodeled bath, the shower is enclosed not by a tiled wall, but by one made of glass block that allows light to reach the stall interior while preserving personal privacy.

Like the kitchen, the bath is being redesigned to meet the needs of individuals having different fitness levels. For example, getting in and out of the tub poses a challenge for those with limited mobility or impaired eyesight. New units are available with lower walls so that stepping in and out is less of a challenge. Attractively designed grab bars placed in strategic locations ease movement around the bathroom.

Large, open shower units, in both custom and stock designs, enable people in wheelchairs to bathe independently. Fold-down seats in the shower are a convenience and a safety feature for anyone, not just the less-mobile members of the household. Pedestal sinks not only lend a sense of style, but free up floor space, allowing people in wheelchairs to get closer to the lavatory to facilitate use. The same applies to wall-hung storage cabinets, which can be installed at any height that's convenient. In small baths, this type of cabinetry also increases a feeling of spaciousness. Slip-resistant finishes applied to floor tiles and tub bottoms help prevent falls, a significant cause of injuries within the home.

While these are fairly substantial changes, smaller adjustments can also increase safety in the bath. Rounded, as opposed to sharp, corners on bath cabinetry and countertops are always a plus. Those with arthritis find that cabinet doors are easier to open when they are fitted with lever handles instead of knobs, and faucets with lever-type handles are likewise easier to operate. Finally, don't forget antiscald regulators to eliminate surges of unpleasantly cold or dangerously hot water in the shower.

CHAPTER EIGHT

PLAYING

The easy relationship between indoors and out in today's homes has blurred distinctions between the two. After hiding indoors in air-conditioned comfort for several decades, we now spend a significant amount of our leisure time outdoors.

Air-conditioning and the automobile may have doomed the front porch to virtual extinction, but many people still mourn the loss of a spacious area where they can sit and watch the world pass by. Indeed, the importance of this space in drawing neighbors together has inspired a sort of front-porch revival in new communities.

At the same time, families have turned to the backyard to enjoy the outdoors in relative privacy. The small service porch at the back of the typical pre–World War II house is but a memory. Long ago, those porches were replaced by patios, decks, and terraces that enable us to relax outside and savor the fresh air and sunshine on a seasonal basis.

In most cases, adding an outdoor living area is a cost-effective home improvement. Besides being a relatively inexpensive project, the addition often pays for itself by increasing the value of the house. And many families don't settle for just one such addition. Decks in particular are so popular that it's not unusual to see them extending off the family room, the dining room, and the master suite of the same house.

People have begun to think of outdoor living and dining areas as open-air rooms to be furnished much like indoor spaces. The heavy, rust-prone, wrought-iron furniture of the

Pages 126–127: Bridging the divide between indoors and out, the screened porch expands usable living space at a reasonable cost. Notice how the twig furnishings in this example further blur the distinction between the interior setting and the natural landscape.
Right: The deck has become a backyard institution with homeowners using it as a second family room and/or dining room. Durable wooden furnishings, which complement the shingled exterior of the house, beckon the entire family to cook and dine outdoors in the fresh air.

Opposite: On this peaceful porch, a wicker rocking chair soothes occupants with its lulling motion, while a hammock invites lounging and even napping. An occasional table and a stool, both in white wicker, provide convenient spots for resting drinks and magazines. For those who crave more of an escape—a place where the ring of the phone can't be heard—a gazebo set away from the house offers a sense of seclusion and a slight change of scenery. **Above:** The outdoor kitchen—wildly popular for a short time during the 1950s—is experiencing a comeback, spurred by a renewed interest in making the most of outdoor living space. Although most are simple affairs geared toward grilling, this one takes the form of a full-fledged kitchen. Amenities include a sink, a refrigerator for beverages, and cabinetry with specialized storage. **Right:** Outfitted with garden furnishings, this small brick patio is an ideal spot for a tête-à-tête. Just steps above, a deck plays host to the owner's container garden, which is filled with greenery and cheerful blooms.

past has been supplemented with durable lightweight pieces made from a variety of materials and available in a wide range of design styles. Also available is quick-drying and exceptionally durable upholstery that mimics natural materials. With the addition of a few throw pillows, an outdoor area becomes an inviting place to visit with friends and soak up panoramic views. You can even include a retractable awning on a deck to provide shade when desired.

Cooking outdoors is particularly appealing in warm weather. Here, you can relax with the kids on a casual grilled-burgers night or treat friends to a more sophisticated menu. To prevent dashing back and forth from the house to the grill, some homeowners build an outdoor kitchen with a small refrigerator and work area as well as a little storage space.

Outdoor dining has come a long way since the 1950s, when a casual picnic setting was the rule. Informal dining is still popular, but paper or plastic plates have, in many households, been replaced with pretty earthenware dishes and stylish stainless steel or silverplated flatware. It's not uncommon to see fine linen napkins taken outdoors, where they are joined by cheery floral centerpieces and other indoor accessories. Indeed, some families set the outdoor table with the same fine china and silverware they use in the dining room.

Like their indoor counterparts, outdoor living spaces are often multifunctional. It's easy to make a deck a year-round destination by incorporating a hot tub or sauna for winter pleasure.

Our embrace of nature has revived the notion of building outdoor structures. Who isn't drawn to a romantic gazebo overlooking a pretty garden, or charmed by the idea of a summerhouse—small, enclosed, and consisting of one room—for reading, painting, or hosting a children's tea party? While doubling as a quaint outdoor focal point or destination, a pool or storage shed supplies space for stashing seasonal outdoor furnishings, games, and lawn equipment. Even a simple bench set in a secluded corner of the garden can become a place to rest and meditate.

Left: In many cases, the deck has evolved into a multifunctional space equipped to entertain family and friends both day and night. This one acts as living room, dining room, and private oasis. A fire pit—which extends the use of the area into early autumn—encourages guests and residents to gather around, share stories, and perhaps even sing a few songs. The octagonal arrangement of the built-in benches makes it easier for everyone to talk to and hear one another. For those who want to engage in more intimate conversations, a swing for two (located toward the rear) offers its service. **Right:** A dining table, complete with an umbrella, offers a shady spot for cozy alfresco meals.

It's easy to make a deck a year-round destination by incorporating a hot tub or sauna for winter pleasure.

Left: Steps lead up to a somewhat sheltered hot tub, which offers the ultimate in relaxation. Bench seating around one side of the tub gives those who prefer to stay dry the chance to chat with friends enjoying a soak.

Fortunately, there are many ways to embellish the lawn and garden with an outdoor structure. A number of companies manufacture gazebos and sheds ready to be painted or finished to blend with a particular outdoor scheme. Magazines and books sell blueprints for do-it-yourselfers who want to build their own outdoor retreats. Before you take advantage of that option, check with local authorities, as you may be required to obtain a building permit.

Decorating a summer room or shed is an excellent way to create a reminder of summer that lasts throughout the year. Adirondack and wicker furnishings are inexpensive and charming. There's no need to stick to conventional white. Instead, you can spray-paint pieces dark forest green and black in turn-of-the-century fashion or periwinkle and other cheery colors. Mix these with inexpensive area rugs, candles, and mood-setting accessories, such as pressed leaves and flowers or framed maps, to create a welcoming sitting room. Or let the children claim this area as their very own playhouse. You can even use a summer room or shed as a guest room for youngsters when weekend visitors fill the house. The kids will love the sense of adventure.

Some spaces—call them transitional—bridge the gap between indoors and out. A typical example is the screened porch. With today's emphasis on stylish decorating, you're far more likely to find a comfortable wicker sofa, dining table, and armchairs than a 1950s picnic table and benches. And don't be surprised to see an area rug or draperies. Many screened porches have ceiling fans to stir up a cooling breeze on still summer afternoons, as well as lighting schemes that invite you onto the porch in the evening. You may find relaxing on a screened porch so enjoyable that you opt to enclose it with removable Plexiglas panes, creating a three-season room.

A sunspace, such as a sunroom or an attached greenhouse, functions in much the same way as a screened porch. Eminently adaptable, such a space can become a light and airy sitting or dining area or simply a lush garden to brighten

Below: A latticework trellis subtly separates this outdoor room from the garden. Shady and cool, the space is an inviting spot for enjoying a leisurely weekend lunch. Wicker is a popular choice for outdoor furnishings, as its texture provides a link to the natural surroundings.

Decorating a summer room or shed is an excellent way to create a reminder of summer that lasts throughout the year.

Above: A fanciful playhouse not only gives kids a place that they can call their own, but lends charm to a backyard as well. This private hideaway sports a coat of soft blue paint and white trim. Polka-dotted curtains with cord tiebacks and window boxes filled with bright flowers dress up the facade. Mimicking its larger counterparts, the pint-sized house features a front porch, complete with an amiable rocking chair. **Left:** This sunroom addition extends off the kitchen, opening up the latter and giving it an expansive feel. Furnished as a family room, the sunny space allows friends and family to visit with the cook in comfort.

Opposite: This sunroom has it all—a place to work, a place to daydream, and a place to eat. Plus, it harvests the warmth of the sun, which is then absorbed by a thick concrete floor that has been topped with ceramic tile for decorative purposes. Blinds on the overhead glazing can be closed to provide respite from the sun. With its combination of outdoor ambience and indoor comforts, the space functions as a natural transition between the interior and the deck. **Below:** A conservatory can do triple duty as a nurturing environment for plants, a supplemental living area, and a second dining room. Here, a wooden bench just beyond the doors provides a spot to enjoy the fresh air during the warmer months.

the indoors. In some cases, families move a desk into the sunspace to create a sunny home office. A small auxiliary sitting area is a cozy place for adults to share afternoon coffee with a friend or for children to wrestle with homework at night. Because most sunspaces have durable, ceramic-tile flooring, they can host children's activities quite easily during inclement weather. Of course, these rooms are ideal for nurturing plants. Imagine having the luxury of colorful flowering plants in the dead of winter or growing a kitchen garden that can be harvested all year long.

Most of the time, we think of sunspaces as appropriate only on the first floor of a home. But more and more, they are being incorporated into the second and even third floors of new houses and additions. Some new houses even incorporate sunspaces that soar two stories high. Though this strategy eliminates the potential living area that would be available above a one-story sunspace, a two-story design brightens both floors and promotes the circulation of air and warmth. It also provides room to hang enormous plants—think leafy green ferns—that bring a bit of visual drama.

All too often, sunspaces lose expensive winter heat to the outdoors, which needlessly increases energy bills. But when sited properly along the south side of a home, these spaces harvest direct solar warmth from sunlight, creating a comfortable indoor environment during the day. Homeowners sometimes go a step further and specify a thick concrete slab beneath the floor. This thermal mass, as it is known, absorbs excess solar warmth and releases it slowly at night, thus reducing winter heating costs. Properly sized roof overhangs, shade from nearby trees, and venting prevent the undesirable buildup of summer heat.

With so many options available, there's no reason for our homes to be shut off from sunlight, fresh air, and natural greenery any longer. Just like converting a guest room into a home office or outfitting a kitchen with a dining area, inviting these refreshing elements into our everyday lives makes our homes more habitable, functional, and just plain enjoyable.

Right: In a space that is both sunroom and dining room, fresh herbs for cooking can flourish. Simple wooden furnishings allow the outdoor scenery to take center stage. On the table, a lazy Susan makes serving easier.

With so many options available, there's no reason for our homes to be shut off from sunlight, fresh air, and natural greenery any longer.

Left: Thanks to an addition, this versatile kitchen also acts as a dining area, sitting room, and greenhouse. The cushioned chairs not only encourage lounging, but also infuse the space with a tropical air that complements the abundance of plants. The tile floor picks up the natural greenery and offers a durable, low-maintenance surface—ideal for an area where spills (either from beverages or watering cans) are likely to occur.

Opposite: With its tremendous height and vast expanses of glass, this sunroom makes occupants feel as though they're sitting outside. The rugged wood beams used for the framework enhance the natural feel of the setting, as do the potted plants. Outfitted with comfortable seating and a durable terra-cotta tile floor, the space is perfect for no-fuss entertaining. A painted trunk finds new life as a coffee table, its weathered appearance in keeping with the surroundings.

SOURCE DIRECTORY

BATHROOMS/KITCHENS

American Standard
(800) 524-9797 ext. 886
www.americanstandard.com

Avonite
(800) 4-AVONITE

Corian
(800) 4-CORIAN

Creative Surface Solutions
4720 Quality Court
Las Vegas, NV 89103
(702) 365-6444

Elkay
90 Hedgedale Rd.
Brampton, Ontario
Canada L6T 5L2
(630) 574-8484
(800) 661-1795 (Canada only)
www.elkay.com

Home Depot
(800) 430-3376 (U.S.)
(800) 668-2266 (Canada)
www.homedepot.com

Jacuzzi
(800) 288-4002
www.jacuzzi.com

Kohler
(800) 4-KOHLER
www.kohlerco.com

KWC Faucets
(888) 592-3287

Moen
(877) DRINK-H20
www.moen.com

Price Pfister
(800) PFaucet
www.pricepfister.com

St. Thomas Creations
(619) 336-3980
www.stthomascreations.com

CABINETRY

Amera Fine Cabinetry by
　Merillet
(800) 895-7314

Aristokraft Cabinetry
1 Masterbrand Cabinet Drive
Jasper, IN 47456
(812) 482-2527

Hafele America
(800) 423-3531

Home Depot
(800) 430-3376 (U.S.)
(800) 668-2266 (Canada)
www.homedepot.com

Ikea
(800) 434-IKEA

KraftMaid Cabinetry
P.O. Box 1055
1052 Industrial Parkway
Middlefield, OH 44062
(440) 632-5333
www.kraftmaid.com

Neil Kelly Cabinets
804 North Alberta Street
Portland, OR 97217
(503) 288-NEIL

Plain and Fancy Custom
　Cabinetry
(800) 447-9006

Rutt Custom Cabinetry
(800) 220-RUTT
www.rutt1.com

Siematic
(800) 355-8221

Snaidero
201 West 132nd Street
Los Angeles, CA 90061
(310) 516-8499
www.snaiderousa.com

Wellborn
(800) 336-8040

William Laberge Cabinetmaker
5145 Rte. 30
Dorset, VT 05251
(802) 325-2117
www.vtweb.com/laberge/

Wood-Mode Cabinetry
1 Second Street
Kreamer, PA 17833
(570) 374-2711

FLOORING/FLOOR COVERINGS

Alloc
(877) DO-ALLOC
www.alloc.com

Armstrong Floors
(888) ARMSTRONG

Bruce Hardwood Floors
(800) 722-4647

Busby-Gilbert Tile Co.
16021 Arminta Street
Van Nuys, CA 91406
(818) 780-9460

Carpet Express
(800) 922-5582

Country Floors
New York, NY
(212) 627-8300
Los Angeles, CA
(310) 657-0510

Dal-Tile
(800) 933-TILE

Dupee Antique Flooring
(800) 231-1353

Dupont Carpeting
(800) 4-DUPONT

Goodwin Heart Pine Co.
106 SW 109th Place
Micanopy, FL 32667
(800) 336-3118

Home Depot
(800) 430-3376 (U.S.)
(800) 668-2266 (Canada)
www.homedepot.com

Italian Tile Center
Division of the Italian Trade
　Commission
499 Park Avenue
New York, NY 10022
(212) 980-1500

Karastan Carpets
(800) 234-1120
www.karastan.com

Mannington Resilient Floors
(800) FLOOR-US
www.mannington.com

Mohawk Carpets
(800) 2-MOHAWK

Nourison
(800) 223-1110

Pergo
(800) 33-PERGO

Wood Flooring America
(877) 966-3356
www.woodflooringamerica.com

FURNITURE

Ballard Design
(800) 284-5116

Basset
(800) 233-7191
www.bassetfurniture.com

The Bombay Company
(800) 829-7789

Broyhill Furniture Industries
(800) 3-BROYHILL

Century Furniture
(800) 852-5552

Charles P. Rogers Brass &
Iron Beds
55 West 17th Street
New York, NY 10011
(800) 272-7726

Crate & Barrel
(800) 323-5461

Drexel Heritage Furnishings
(800) 916-1986

Ethan Allen
(800) 228-9229

French Country Living
10205 Colvin Run Road
Great Falls, VA 22066
(800) 485-1302

Ikea
(800) 434-IKEA

Lexington Furniture Industries
(800) LEX-INFO

Maine Cottage
(207) 846-1430
www.mainecottage.com

Marion Travis
(800) 806-2398
www.mariontravis.com

Mitchell Gold Co.
(800) 789-5401

Pier 1 Imports
(800) 447-4371
www.pier1.com

Rejuvenation Lamp &
Fixture Co.
(888) 343-8548

Rowe Furniture
(800) 334-ROWE ext. 100

Spiegal
(800) 345-4500

Thomasville
401 East Main Street
Thomasville, NC 27361
(800) 650-1669

OUTDOOR FURNISHINGS & FIXTURES

Casablanca Fan Company
761 Corporate Center Drive
Pomona, CA 91768
(888) 227-2178

Country Casual
(800) 284-8325
www.countrycasual.com

Fran's Wicker & Rattan
Furniture
295 Route 10
Succasunna, NJ 07876
(800) 531-1511

Frontera
(800) 762-5374
www.frontera.com

Vermont Outdoor Furniture
(800) 588-8834

PAINT/WALLCOVERING

Benjamin Moore
(800) 826-2623

Blonder
(800) 321-4070

Cabot Stain
(800) US-STAIN

Eisenhart
(800) 931-WALL

Mirage Wallpaper
(800) 366-1701

Sherwin Williams
(800) 4-SHERWIN
www.sherwinwilliams.com

Waverly
(800) 423-5881

York Wallpaper & Fabrics
(800) 375-YORK

SUNROOMS AND CONSERVATORIES

Amdega and Machin
Conservatories
3515 Lakeshore Drive
St. Joseph, MI 49085
(800) 922-0110

Four Seasons Sunrooms
5005 Veterans Highway
Holbrook, NY 11741
(800) 368-7732

Hartford Conservatories, Inc.
96A Commerce Way
Woburn, MA 01801
(800) 963-8700

Screen Tight Porch Screening
System
407 St. James Street
Georgetown, SC 29440
(800) 768-7325

WINDOWS/DOORS

Andersen
(800) 426-4261
www.andersenwindows.com

Home Depot
(800) 430-3376 (U.S.)
(800) 668-2266 (Canada)
www.homedepot.com

Hunter Douglas
(800) 32-STYLE
www.hunterdouglas.com

Kolbe & Kolbe
(800) 955-8177

Loewen Windows
(800) 245-2295 (U.S.)
(800) 563-9367 (Canada)

Marvin
(800) 268-7644
www.marvin.com

Pella
(800) 54-PELLA
www.pellacorporation.com

Pozzi
(800) 257-9663

Velux
(800) 283-2831

Weather Shield
(800) 477-6808

PHOTO CREDITS

©Laurie Black: pp. 13 bottom, 58 bottom, 109 top & bottom

©Judith Bromley: p. 29 top

©Steven Brooke: pp. 12–13, 30 top, 45, 60–61, 99 bottom left & right, 101, 121 bottom

©Grey Crawford: pp. 90–91, 91 bottom

©Steve Cridland: p. 19

©David Frazier: pp. 27, 53 top, 88 bottom, 118–119

©Michael Garland: p. 135 top (designed by Tumbleweeds)

©Susan Gilmore/Esto: pp. 86, 87, 95, 100, 110 left, 120, 123

©Tria Giovan: pp. 30 bottom, 54, 83, 98–99 top, 139

©Kari Haavisto: pp. 51, 56–57, 57 bottom, 89, 107, 135 bottom

©Nancy Hill: pp. 47 bottom, 52–53, 65, 80, 115, 116 (designed by Grant Larkin), 121 top, 137

©Timothy Hursley: pp. 32–33

©Michael Jensen: pp. 2, 10 top, 10 bottom, 10–11, 32 top, 50, 55 bottom, 68–69, 69 bottom

©Jessie Walker & Associates: pp. 75 bottom right, 131 top

©Donna Kempner: p. 44 (Patricia Motzkin, Architect)

©Larry Lambrecht: p. 75 top (Mark P. Finlay Architects)

©Tim Lee: p. 70–71

©David Livingston: pp. 17, 24–25, 26, 31, 34, 37, 42, 52 bottom, 53 bottom, 75 bottom left, 106 bottom, 114, 117 top, 118, 122 bottom

©Ray Main/Mainstream: p. 20 (Chris Cowper, Architect)

©Deborah Mazzoleni: pp. 22, 23 (Mitchell Gold/Bob Williams, homeowners)

©Kit Morris: p. 117 bottom (Dan Phipps & Associates, Architect)

©Keith Scott Morton: pp. 59, 122 top, 125, 138 top & bottom

©Eric Roth: pp. 8-9 (Interior design by Dina Hamilbury), 18, 20-21 (Kalman Construction), 35 top (Weston Hewitson Architects Inc.), 43 (Design by Anne Lenox, Partners in Design), 46–47 (CLC Interiors), 74 top (Design by Anne Lenox, Partners in Design), 74 bottom (Dewing+Schmid Architects), 78–79 (Berg Howland Associates), 85 right (Design by Martin Potter, M.J. Berries), 105 top (Martin Kuckly Associates), 105 bottom (Interior design by Carole Kaplan, Two By Two), 134

©Brad Simmons/Esto: pp. 40, 40–41, 48 top & bottom, 49, 77, 84, 92–93

©Brad Simmons Photography: pp. 58 top (McClenaghan, homeowners), 62 top (Hazen, homeowners; Town & Country Homes; styled by Cindy Martin), 62–63 (Hazen, homeowners; Town & Country Homes; styled by Cindy Martin), 66–67 (Marino, homeowners; Town & Country homes; styled by Cindy Martin), 72 (Campbell, homeowners; Stephen Dynia Architects; styled by Joetta Moulden), 73 (Campbell, homeowner; Stephen Dynia Architects; styled by Joetta Moulden), 76 (Gold, homeowners; built by Yankee Barn Homes; designed by Toad Hall; styled by Joetta Moulden), 81 (Wray, homeowners; built by Mill Creek Post & Beam; styled by Joetta Moulden), 85 left (Taylor, homeowners), 96 (Allison, homeowners; designed by Allison & Associates; styled by Cindy Martin; built by Real Log Homes), 102–103 (Clark, homeowners; built by Real Log Homes), 104 (Built by Timberpeg), 108 (Crowson, homeowners; designed by Spradley Interiors; styled by Joetta Moulden), 112–113; 124 (King, homeowners; built by Real Log Homes; styled by Joetta Moulden), 126–127 (Araujo, homeowners; designed by Evi's Country Snippets; styled by Joetta Moulden), 130 (Bundy, homeowners), 131 bottom (Bowles, homeowners), 132–133 (Goodridge, homeowners; built by Greg Staley; designed by Barry Wehrman; styled by Cindy Martin), 133 top & bottom (Goodridge, homeowners; built by Greg Staley; designed by Barry Wehrman; styled by Cindy Martin)

©Tim Street-Porter: p. 28

©Brian Vanden Brink: pp. 4–5 (Rob Whitten, Architect), 6–7, 14–15 (Scholz & Barclay, Architects), 16 (Warren Hall, Architect), 35 bottom (Elliot & Elliot, Architects), 36 (Loyi Chan, Architect), 55 top (Scott Simons, Architect), 70 top (John Martin, Architect), 82–83 (Pete Bethanis, Architect), 88 top (Centerbrook Architects), 94 (Tom Cataland, Architect), 96–97 top, 97 bottom, 103 (Interior design by Karin Thomas), 106 top (Elliot & Elliot, Architect), 110–111 (Interior design by Susan Thorne) 136 (John Morris, Architect)

©Alan Weintraub: p. 64, 128–129

INDEX